New Classic Quilt Designs

by

Michal Mussell

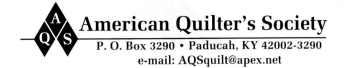

American Quilter's Society
P. O. Box 3290 • Paducah, KY 42002-3290
e-mail: AQSquilt@apex.net

Located in Paducah, Kentucky, the American Quilter's Society (AQS) is dedicated to promoting the accomplishments of today's quilters. Through its publications and events, AQS strives to honor today's quiltmakers and their work and to inspire future creativity and innovation in quiltmaking.

EDITOR: BONNIE K. BROWNING

BOOK DESIGN/ILLUSTRATIONS: MICHAL MUSSELL AND ANGELA SCHADE

COVER DESIGN: MICHAEL BUCKINGHAM

Library of Congress Cataloging-in-Publication Data

Mussell, Michal.

New classic quilt designs / Michal Mussell

p. cm.

Includes bibliographical references (p. 7).

ISBN 1-57432-735-6

1. Patchwork Patterns. 2. Patchwork quilts. I. Title.

TT835.M89 1999

746.46'041--dc21

99-39939

CIP

Additional copies of this book may be ordered from the American Quilter's Society, PO Box 3290, Paducah, KY 42002-3290 @ $19.95. Add $2.00 for postage and handling.

Contents

Introduction

My attraction to quilts has always been the pattern and texture created by the repeat of the quilt block across the surface of the quilt. It is what I enjoy most about traditional quilts.

The experience of a quilt should be one of discovery, a discovery over time, a discovery that continues with each viewing because you can always find something new.

What I offer through my designs is a personal expression of pattern and new variations of visual texture with roots in tradition. I wish for other quilters to discover and enjoy a visual experience of pattern and texture.

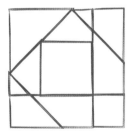 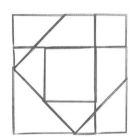 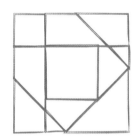 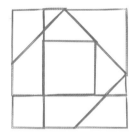

Dedication

To Dennis Tooley – thank you.

To Linda Frihart, Karen Fankhauser, Debi Rankin, Linda Rybnick and others of the Little Balkans Quilt Guild in Pittsburg, Kansas, without your encouragement and support through some difficult times, this would not have been possible.

To Pieter and Winter – you are good kids.

How To Use This Book

This is a b... ...featuring 14 new block ... ...t you have knowledge o... ...quilts may be constructed... ...non-traditional method. I... ...are easily adapted to ... ...ewing techniques. You ... ...ction method that works ...

For traditional method... ...tracing the pattern piec... ...and sewing methods wil... ...sure the pattern pieces an... ...ter and plastic ruler to cut th...

The patterns are labeled alp... ...order in which they will be sew... ...a letter indicates reversing the pa... ...is an "exploded" version of the blo... ...visual tool showing, at a glance, th... ...the block by units.

The cutting dimensions are given for t... ...ings, the setting squares, and the borde... ...borders are cut from the lengthwise grain f... ...greatest stability. Be sure to allow for the borders if they are to be cut from one of the fabrics used in the quilt blocks. When cutting small pieces from a fabric used for borders, cut along the lengthwise grain so you do not cut off the border length.

Please note that the yardages are given for the length of binding needed to go around the edge of the quilt and not for the amount of fabric to buy. I give the information this way because quilters have preferences for the width of binding, double or single fold, and the application method. These factors all affect the amount of fabric to buy to make your own binding.

You can choose fabrics by using the given color scheme or by using the value scheme. "Value" means the lightness or darkness of a fabric. You could also choose one special fabric and then build your other fabric choices around it. These supporting fabrics should accent the main fabric.

A number of the quilts feature large pattern pieces. If you use a special fabric for the large pieces, you can show off that wonderful print ...are loath to cut. Or you could do the opposite...and choose to put a calm print in the area to ...off your quilting skills. The large pieces are ...eat places to add appliqué.

...ilts, I think a balance of visual texture is ...t. Try to establish movement or rhythm ...your quilt. I like to direct the eye as it moves, finding places for it to rest, but not stop, on its journey across the quilt top.

If you prefer, you can use this book to just enjoy the visual sensation of the quilt images. Don't worry about making a quilt. I have more quilt books than time to make all the quilts that I am attracted to. I like to take my favorite quilt books off the shelf and just look at the images, because I enjoy the visual satisfaction. Isn't that what quilts are about – form beyond function?

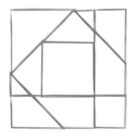
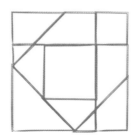
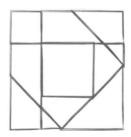
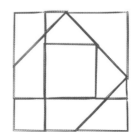

Designing the Quilts

You don't need a computer to design quilts. The computer just aids the decision-making process by showing you alternatives and choices quickly. However, the amount of information can be daunting, so the computer can be a help or a hindrance. Like anything else, using a computer takes practice and education.

DESIGNING WITH A COMPUTER

- Begin with a traditional quilt block. I used square within a square.
- Draw the quilt block using a software program such as Adobe® Illustrator, a precise vector graphics-based program.
- After drawing the block, save the image and then open it in Adobe® Photoshop. Photoshop is a bitmap-based computer program.
- In Photoshop, use the square or the rectangle selection tool to isolate interesting sections of the quilt block.
- Copy and paste the selection into a new document and print it.
- Using the printout, draw the sections you like as new block designs in a quilt design program, such as Quilt-Pro.
- Now you can arrange the new blocks quickly and add color to them.
- Save your favorite designs and print them.
- Use these printouts to choose fabrics.

DESIGNING WITHOUT A COMPUTER

It is possible to replicate the steps to design this book's quilts without a computer. Draw a quilt block on paper. Isolate sections of interest by covering the drawing with blank sheets of paper to outline square or rectangular portions of the block. Draw these areas of interest on another piece of paper to use as new blocks. Draw the new blocks several times or use a copy machine. Cut out and arrange the copies to form quilt designs. Glue the quilt designs to a sheet of paper. The use of grid paper is helpful for arranging the blocks into rows and for adding elements, such as sashing. Make copies of the final quilt design to color with colored pencils or markers. You could also color the blocks before arranging and gluing them.

ADDING SCANNED FABRICS TO THE QUILT DESIGNS

To create the fabric quilt images on the computer, I noted the actual size of the quilts in Quilt-Pro, then exported the quilt designs to Illustrator. In Illustrator, I scaled the quilts from the actual finished size to fit on a page, taking special note of the scale percentage. I then saved the images. The Illustrator program will also save the images with "paths" that can be used in Photoshop. Paths are the mathematical, vector information the computer uses to describe the geometric shapes.

In Photoshop, the fabrics were scanned, using the scale percentage consistent with the scale of the quilt designs I had saved in Illustrator. For example, if the quilt designs were scaled to 20% of the actual size, then the fabrics were scaled to

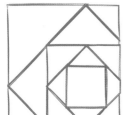
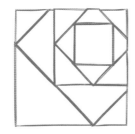
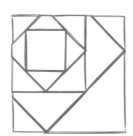
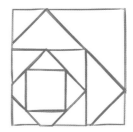

20% also. The fabric images were saved in separate document files, then the quilt designs were opened using the "as paths" option. By opening the images as "paths", I was able to select the "paths" and turn them into selection marquees. This method saved time and computer memory. Once a patch selection in the quilt design was made, I opened a fabric document. In the fabric document, the fabric image was selected and copied. In the quilt design image, the fabric image was pasted into the selection. I continued this select, select, copy, and paste routine until the designs were complete. Then the final images were saved and printed.

I use an Apple Macintosh computer. It is a Power PC 7500/100 with 128 megabytes of RAM. My printer is a Hewlett-Packard DeskJet 855C, and my scanner is a UMAX Astra 600S.

Resources

Adobe Systems, Inc.
345 Park Avenue
San Jose, CA 95110-2704
800-879-3219
www.adobe.com

Apple Computers, Inc.
1 Infinite Loop
Cupertino, CA 95014-2084
408-996-10210
www.apple.com

Hewlett-Packard Co.
P.O. Box 3025
Corvallis, OR 97339
208-323-2551
www.hp.com

Quilt-Pro Systems, Inc.
P.O. Box 560692
The Colony, TX 75056
800-884-1511
www.quiltpro.com

UMAX Technologies, Inc.
3561 Gateway Blvd.
Fremont, CA 94538
510-651-4000
www.umax.com

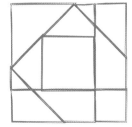 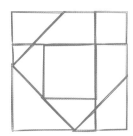 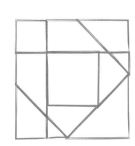 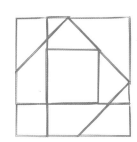

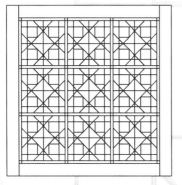

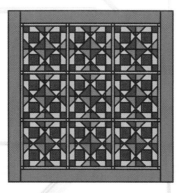

TULIP SQUARES

Use Construction block.

Patterns on pages 11–13

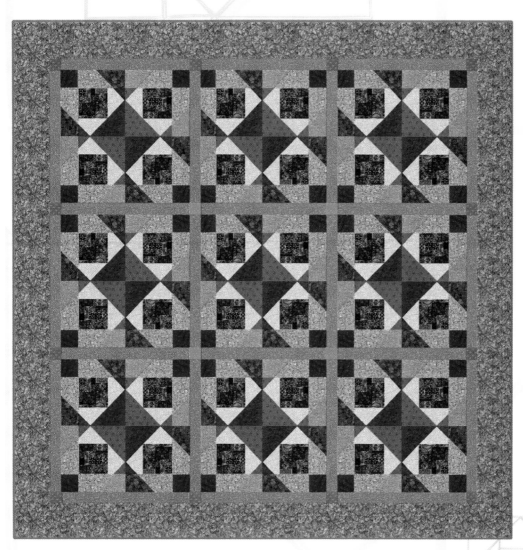

92" x 92" finished size
12" block
1½" sashing
7" border

New Classic Quilt Designs – Michal Mussell

Construction block

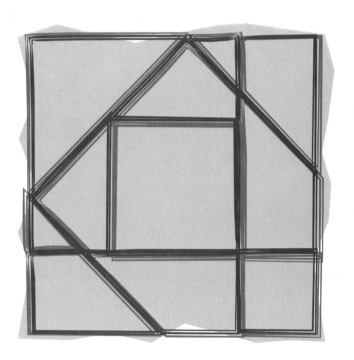

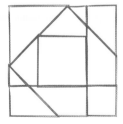 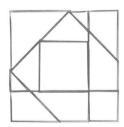 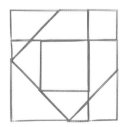

Tulip Squares Yardages

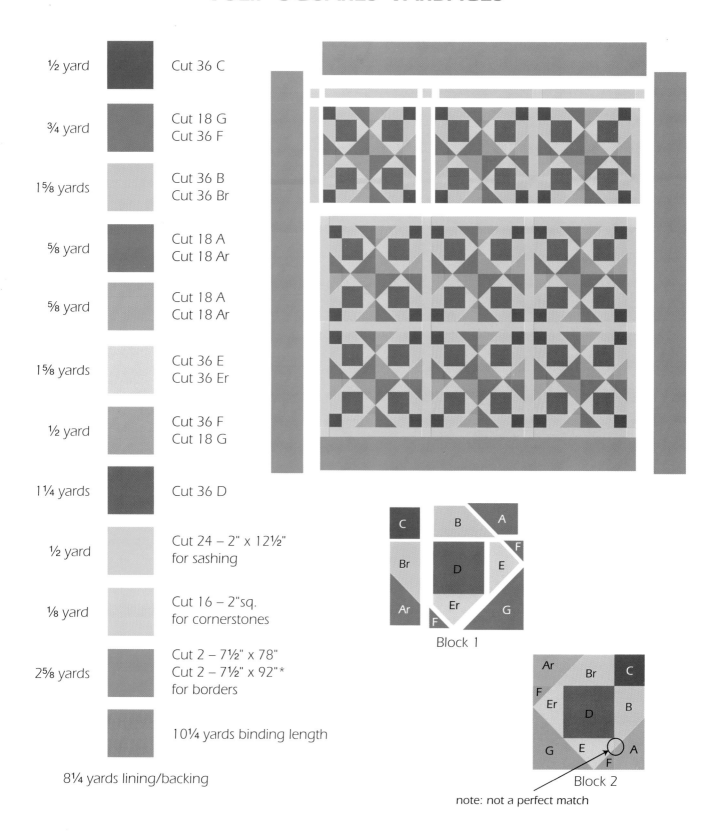

½ yard — Cut 36 C

¾ yard — Cut 18 G / Cut 36 F

1⅝ yards — Cut 36 B / Cut 36 Br

⅝ yard — Cut 18 A / Cut 18 Ar

⅝ yard — Cut 18 A / Cut 18 Ar

1⅝ yards — Cut 36 E / Cut 36 Er

½ yard — Cut 36 F / Cut 18 G

1¼ yards — Cut 36 D

½ yard — Cut 24 – 2" x 12½" for sashing

⅛ yard — Cut 16 – 2"sq. for cornerstones

2⅝ yards — Cut 2 – 7½" x 78" / Cut 2 – 7½" x 92"* for borders

10¼ yards binding length

8¼ yards lining/backing

Block 1

Block 2

note: not a perfect match

* Always measure quilt top before cutting borders.
Borders are cut on the lengthwise grain.

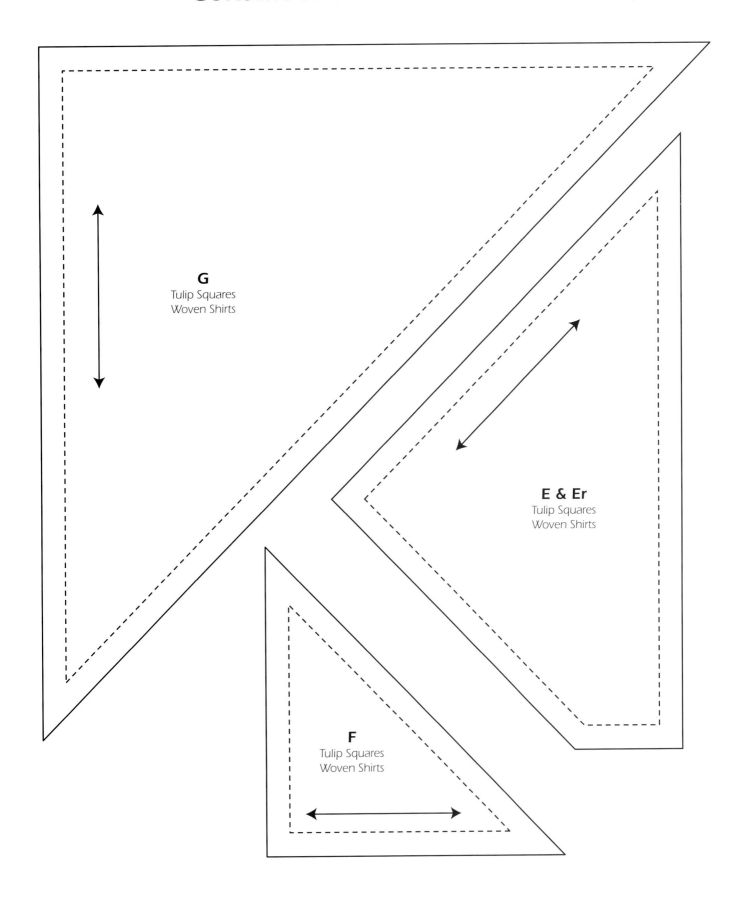

G
Tulip Squares
Woven Shirts

E & Er
Tulip Squares
Woven Shirts

F
Tulip Squares
Woven Shirts

CONSTRUCTION BLOCK PATTERNS

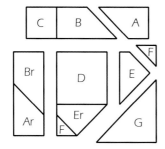 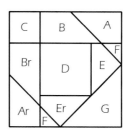

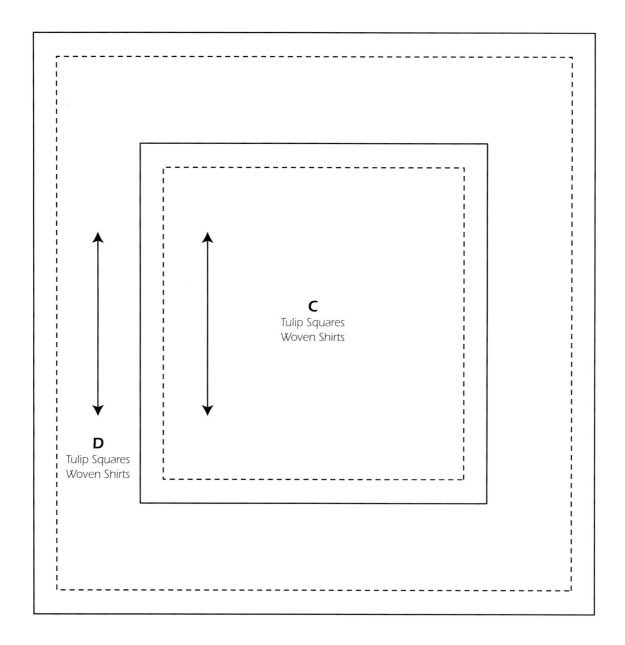

C
Tulip Squares
Woven Shirts

D
Tulip Squares
Woven Shirts

CONSTRUCTION BLOCK PATTERNS

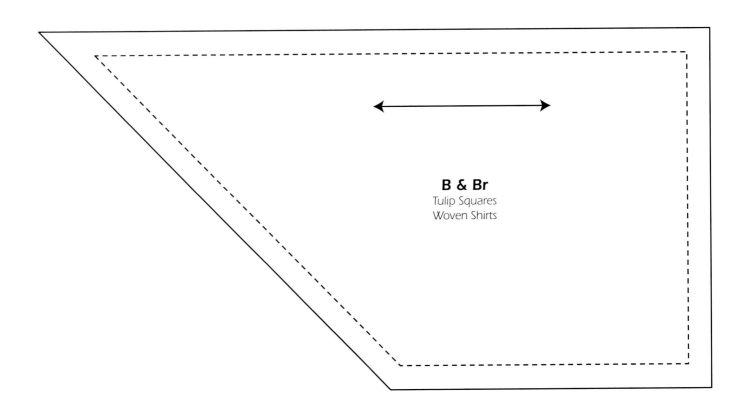

B & Br
Tulip Squares
Woven Shirts

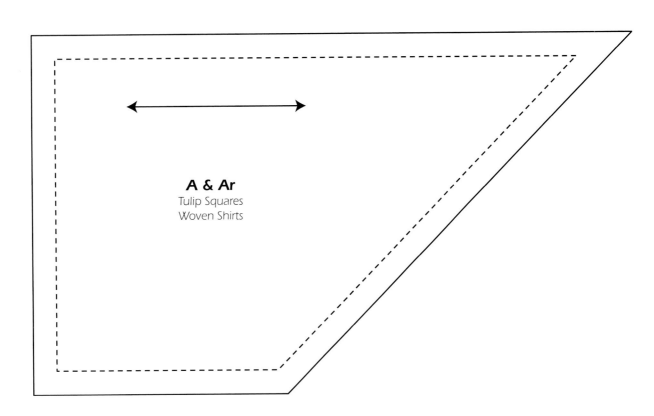

A & Ar
Tulip Squares
Woven Shirts

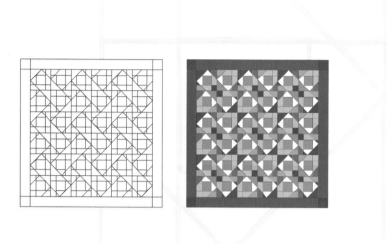

WOVEN SHIRTS

Use Construction block.

Patterns on pages 11–13

84" x 84" finished size
12" block
6" border

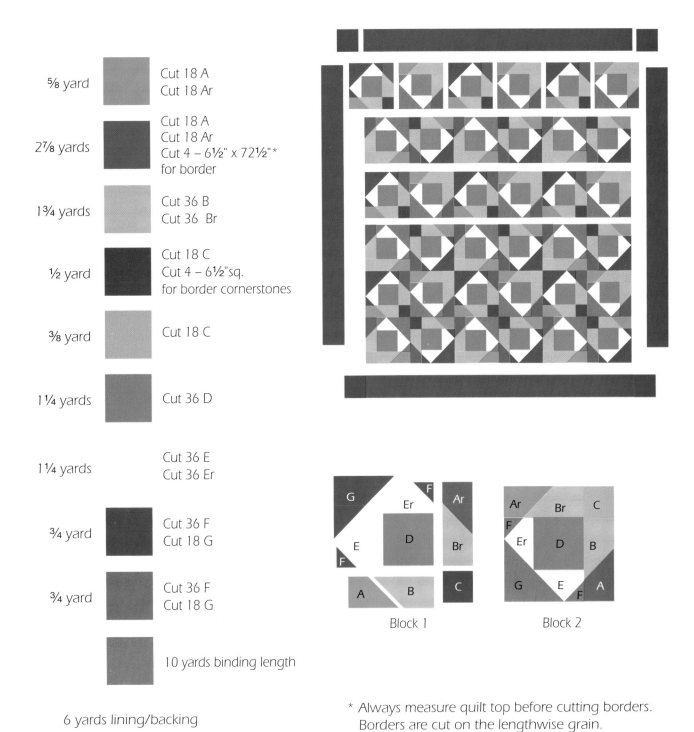

⅝ yard — Cut 18 A / Cut 18 Ar

2⅞ yards — Cut 18 A / Cut 18 Ar / Cut 4 – 6½" x 72½"* for border

1¾ yards — Cut 36 B / Cut 36 Br

½ yard — Cut 18 C / Cut 4 – 6½"sq. for border cornerstones

⅜ yard — Cut 18 C

1¼ yards — Cut 36 D

1¼ yards — Cut 36 E / Cut 36 Er

¾ yard — Cut 36 F / Cut 18 G

¾ yard — Cut 36 F / Cut 18 G

10 yards binding length

6 yards lining/backing

Block 1

Block 2

* Always measure quilt top before cutting borders. Borders are cut on the lengthwise grain.

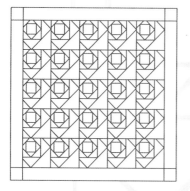 

DRIED FLOWERS

Use In A Corner block.
Patterns on pages 19–21

72" x 72" finished size
12" block
6" border

New Classic Quilt Designs – Michal Mussell

In A Corner block

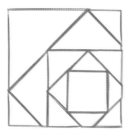 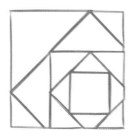 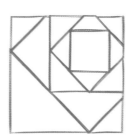

DRIED FLOWERS YARDAGES

½ yard — Cut 13 A

½ yard — Cut 12 A

⅞ yard — Cut 50 B
Cut 50 C

¾ yard — Cut 13 D
Cut 26 F
Cut 13 E

¾ yard — Cut 12 D
Cut 24 F
Cut 12 E

¾ yard — Cut 13 G
Cut 13 Gr
Cut 4 – 6½" sq.
for border cornerstones

⅔ yard — Cut 12 G
Cut 12 Gr

1 yard — Cut 26 F
Cut 13 H

1 yard — Cut 24 F
Cut 12 H

1⅞ yards — Cut 4 – 6½" x 60½"*
for borders

8¼ yards length binding

4½ yards lining/backing

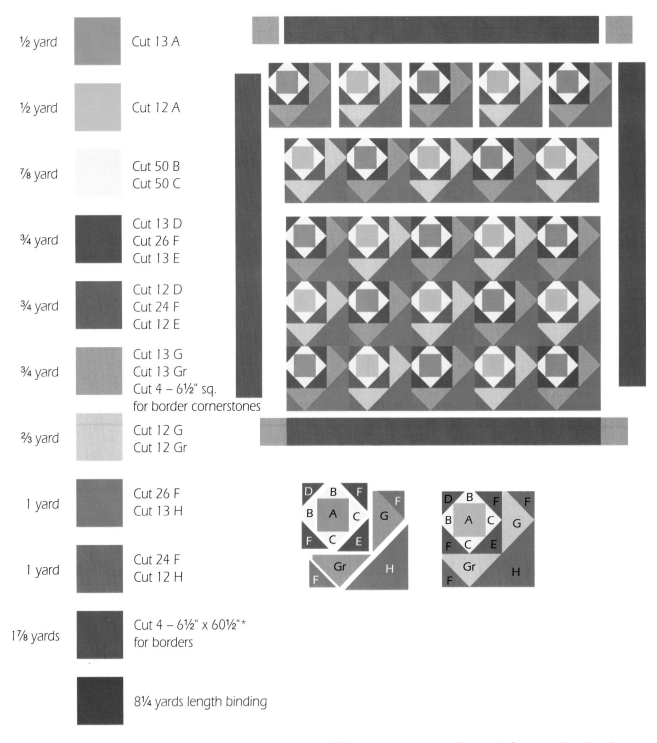

* Always measure quilt top before cutting borders.
Borders are cut on the lengthwise grain.

In A Corner block patterns

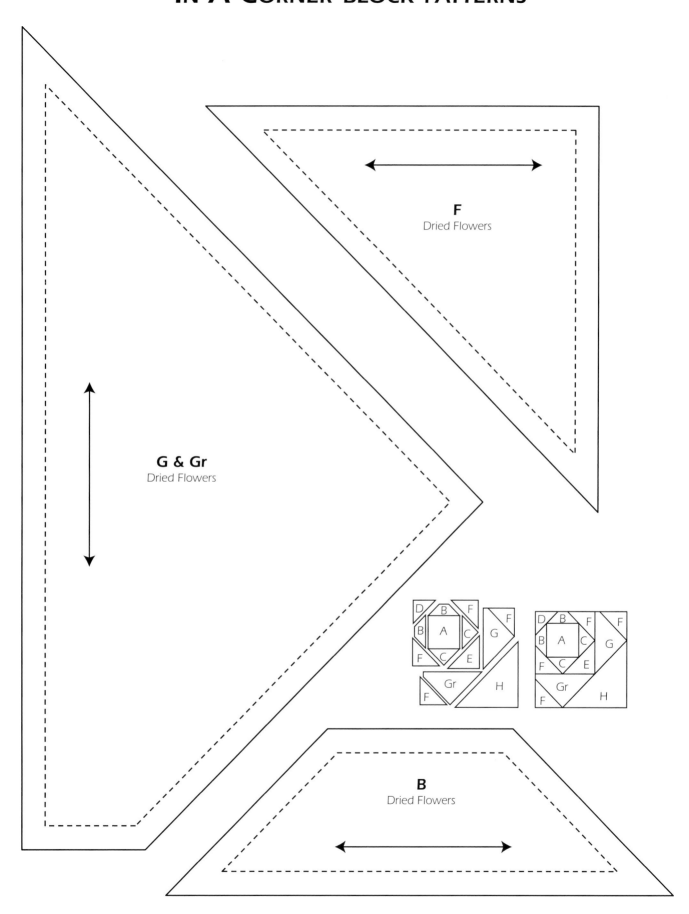

F
Dried Flowers

G & Gr
Dried Flowers

B
Dried Flowers

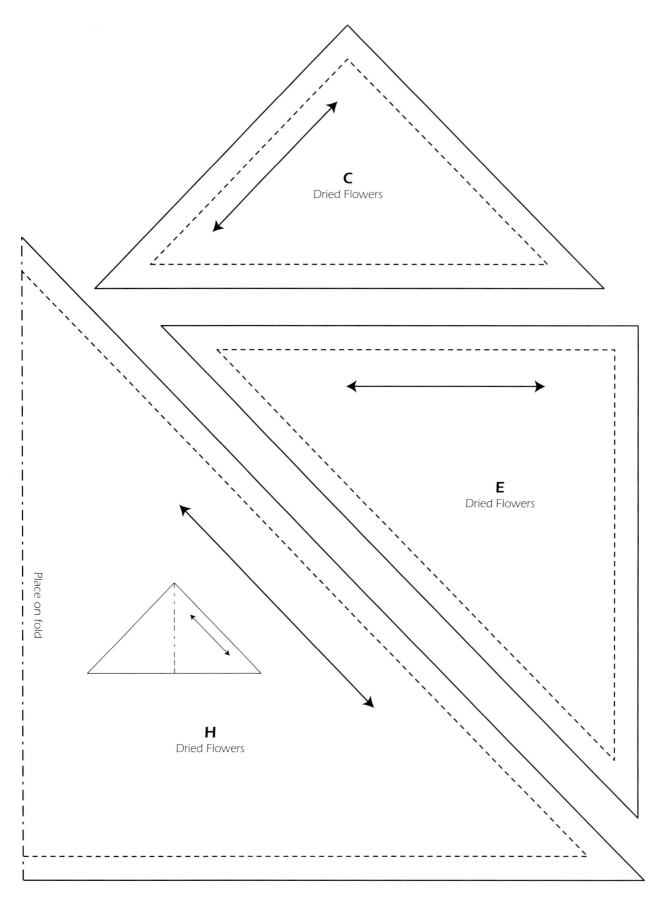

C
Dried Flowers

E
Dried Flowers

Place on fold

H
Dried Flowers

IN A CORNER BLOCK PATTERNS

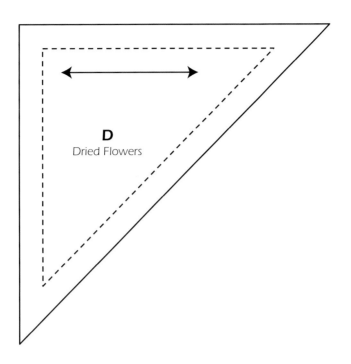

D
Dried Flowers

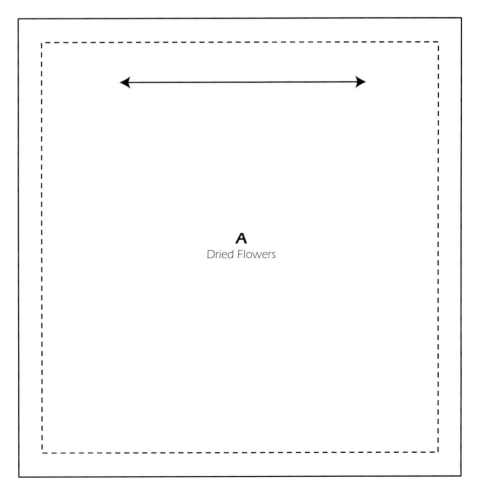

A
Dried Flowers

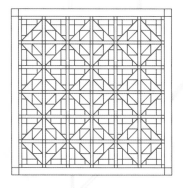

GRANDMA'S SQUARE

Use One Flight Up block.
Patterns on pages 25–27

108" x 108" finished size
14" blocks
2" sashing
5" borders

One Flight Up block

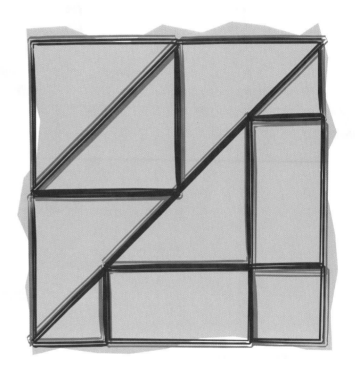

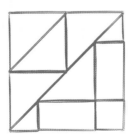 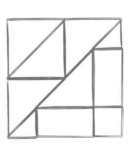 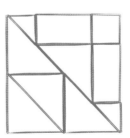

GRANDMA'S SQUARE YARDAGES

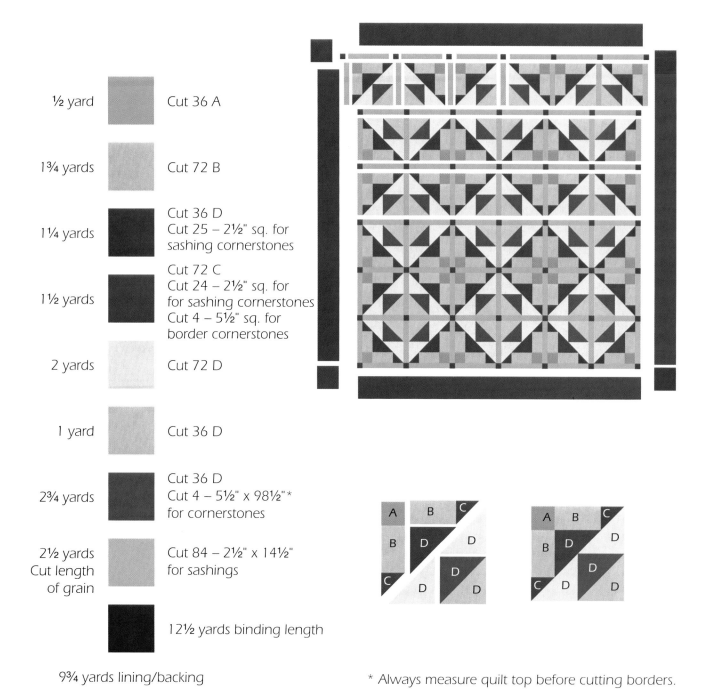

½ yard — Cut 36 A

1¾ yards — Cut 72 B

1¼ yards — Cut 36 D
Cut 25 – 2½" sq. for sashing cornerstones

1½ yards — Cut 72 C
Cut 24 – 2½" sq. for for sashing cornerstones
Cut 4 – 5½" sq. for border cornerstones

2 yards — Cut 72 D

1 yard — Cut 36 D

2¾ yards — Cut 36 D
Cut 4 – 5½" x 98½"* for cornerstones

2½ yards
Cut length of grain — Cut 84 – 2½" x 14½" for sashings

12½ yards binding length

9¾ yards lining/backing

* Always measure quilt top before cutting borders. Borders are cut on the lengthwise grain.

ONE FLIGHT UP BLOCK PATTERNS

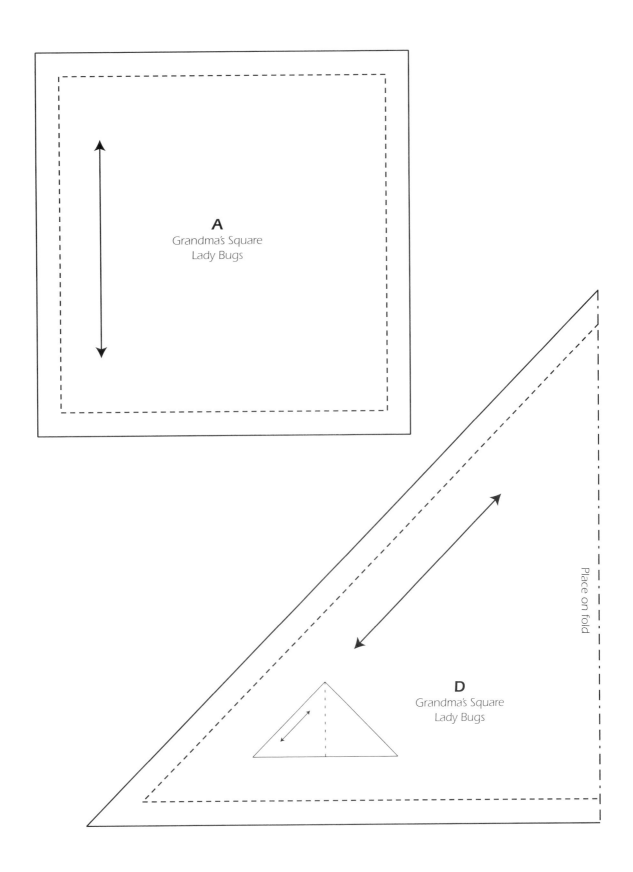

A
Grandma's Square
Lady Bugs

D
Grandma's Square
Lady Bugs

Place on fold

B
Grandma's Square
Lady Bugs

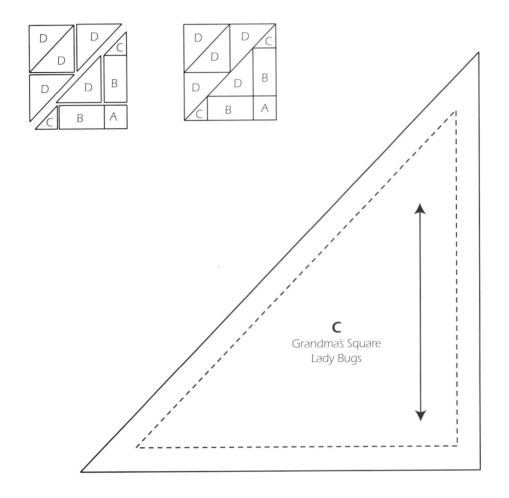

C
Grandma's Square
Lady Bugs

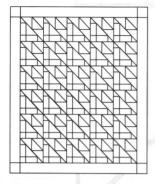

LADY BUGS

Use One Flight Up block.

Patterns on pages 25–27

82" x 96" finished size
14" block
6" border

New Classic Quilt Designs – Michal Mussell

LADY BUGS YARDAGES

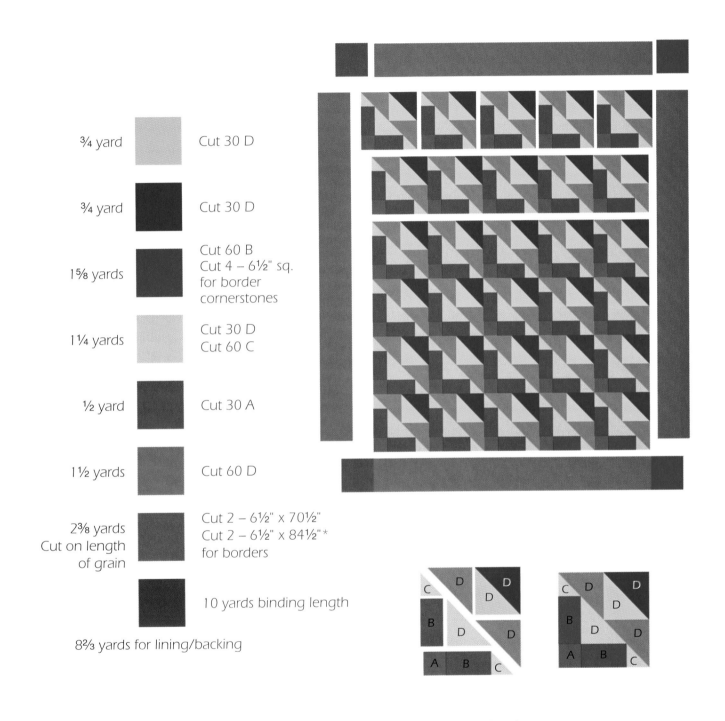

¾ yard — Cut 30 D

¾ yard — Cut 30 D

1⅝ yards — Cut 60 B
Cut 4 – 6½" sq.
for border
cornerstones

1¼ yards — Cut 30 D
Cut 60 C

½ yard — Cut 30 A

1½ yards — Cut 60 D

2⅜ yards
Cut on length
of grain — Cut 2 – 6½" x 70½"
Cut 2 – 6½" x 84½"*
for borders

10 yards binding length

8⅔ yards for lining/backing

* Always measure quilt top before cutting borders.
Borders are cut on the lengthwise grain.

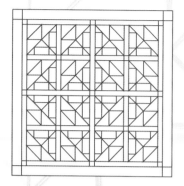

THE SOUND OF TRUMPETS

Use Champagne block.
Patterns on page 33

62" x 62" finished size
12" block
2" sashing
2" & 4" borders

Champagne block

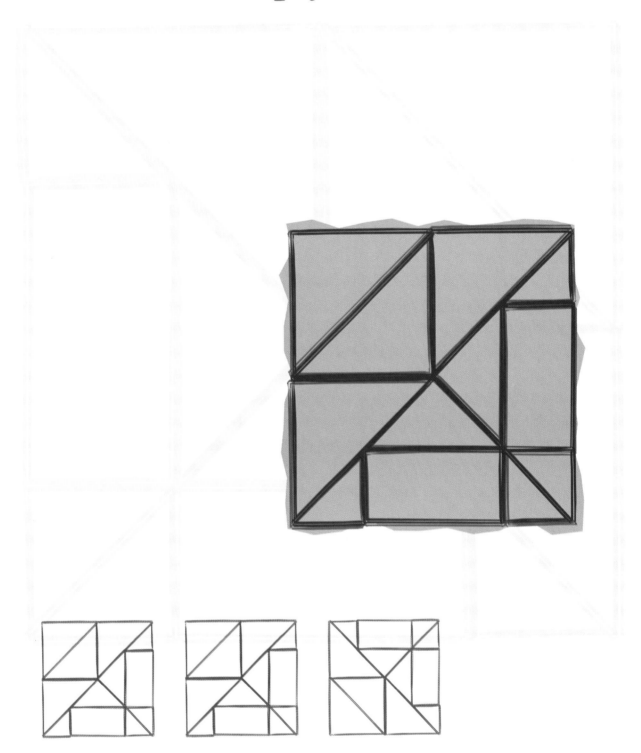

THE SOUND OF TRUMPETS YARDAGES

½ yard — Cut 16 D

½ yard — Cut 16 D

1 yard — Cut 32 D

¾ yard — Cut 16 B
Cut 32 C

¾ yard — Cut 16 B
Cut 32 C
Cut 4 – 4½" sq.
for border
cornerstones

⅞ yard — Cut 32 A

⅛ yard — Cut 13 – 2½" sq.
for sashing cornerstones

1¾ yards — Cut 4 – 4½" x 58½"*
for borders

1⅛ yards — Cut 12 – 2½" x 26½"
Cut 16 – 2½" x 12½"
for sashings

7 yards length of binding

4 yards for lining/backing

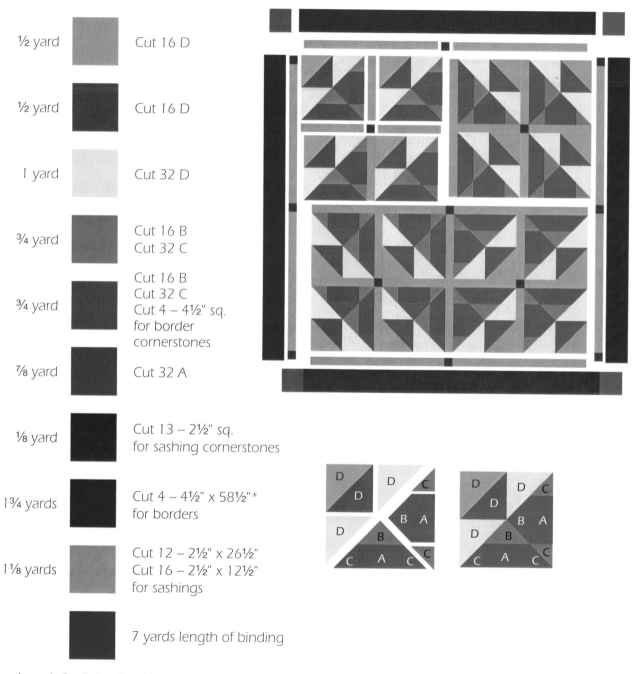

* Always measure quilt top before cutting borders.
  Borders are cut on the lengthwise grain.

CHAMPAGNE BLOCK PATTERNS

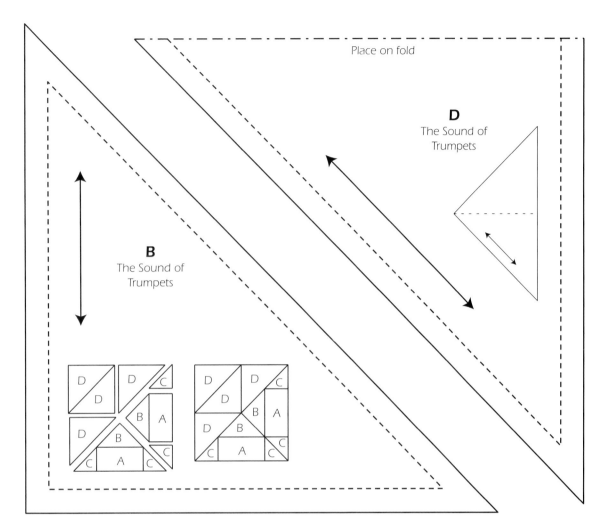

Place on fold

D
The Sound of Trumpets

B
The Sound of Trumpets

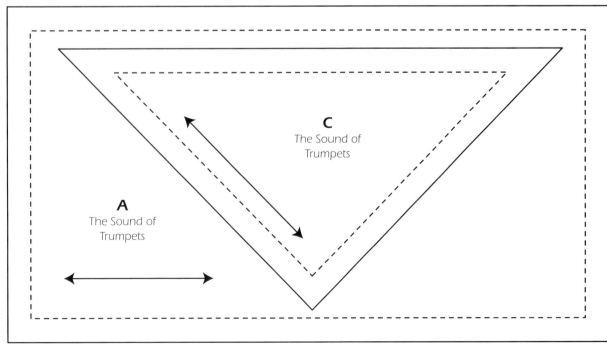

C
The Sound of Trumpets

A
The Sound of Trumpets

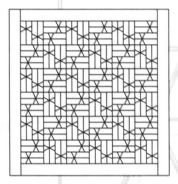

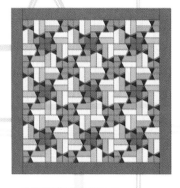

LET'S GO FOR A SPIN

Use Buried Treasure block.

Patterns on page 37

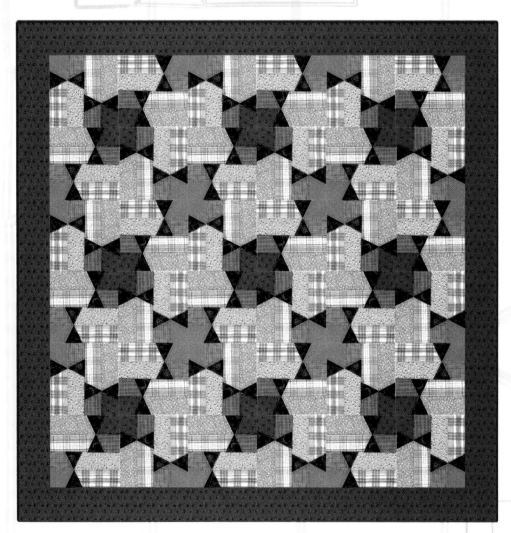

84" x 84" finished size
12" block
6" border

New Classic Quilt Designs – Michal Mussell

Buried Treasure block

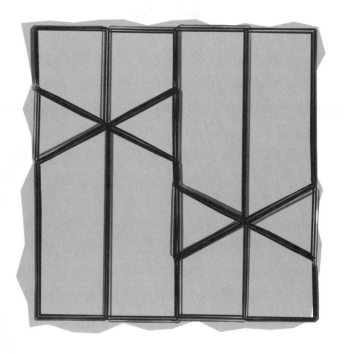

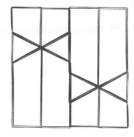 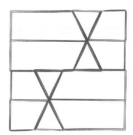 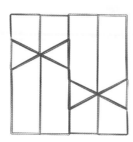

LET'S GO FOR A SPIN YARDAGES

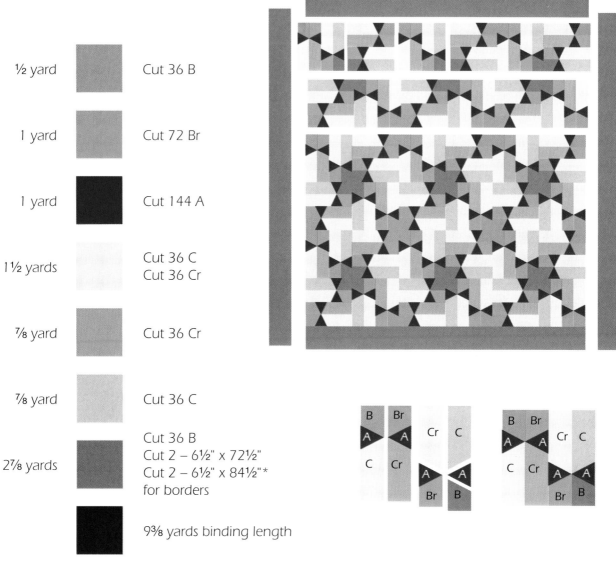

½ yard — Cut 36 B

1 yard — Cut 72 Br

1 yard — Cut 144 A

1½ yards — Cut 36 C
Cut 36 Cr

⅞ yard — Cut 36 Cr

⅞ yard — Cut 36 C

2⅞ yards — Cut 36 B
Cut 2 – 6½" x 72½"
Cut 2 – 6½" x 84½"*
for borders

9⅜ yards binding length

7 yards lining/backing (5 yards if you are careful)

* Always measure quilt top before cutting borders.
Borders are cut on the lengthwise grain.

New Classic Quilt Designs – Michal Mussell

BURIED TREASURE block patterns

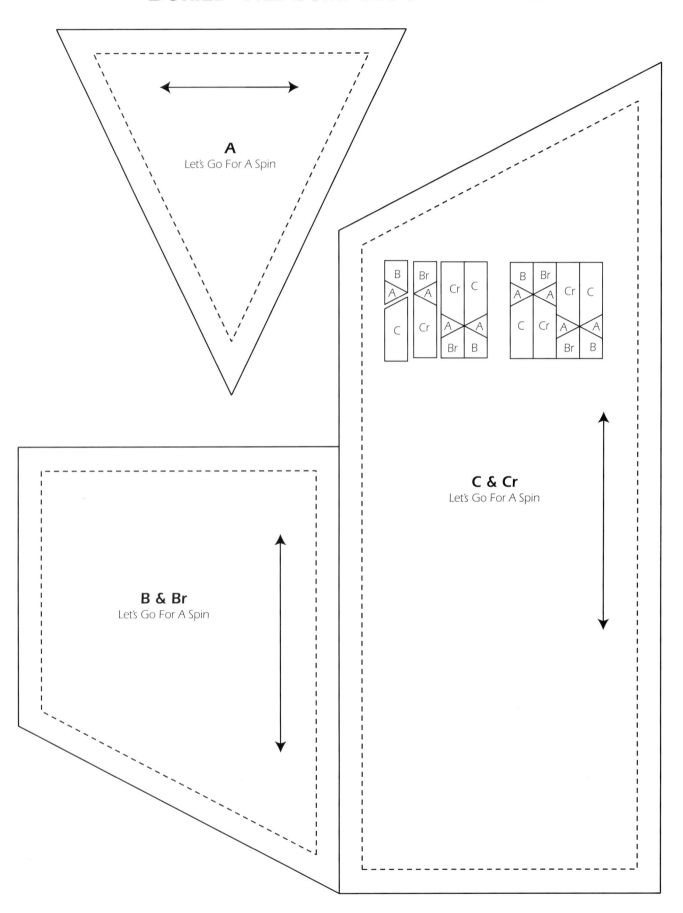

A
Let's Go For A Spin

C & Cr
Let's Go For A Spin

B & Br
Let's Go For A Spin

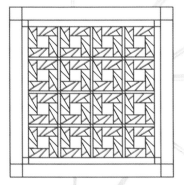

A NEW SPIN

Use Taking Flight block.
Patterns on pages 41–43

92" x 92" finished size
16½" blocks
3½" & 7" borders

New Classic Quilt Designs – Michal Mussell

Taking Flight block

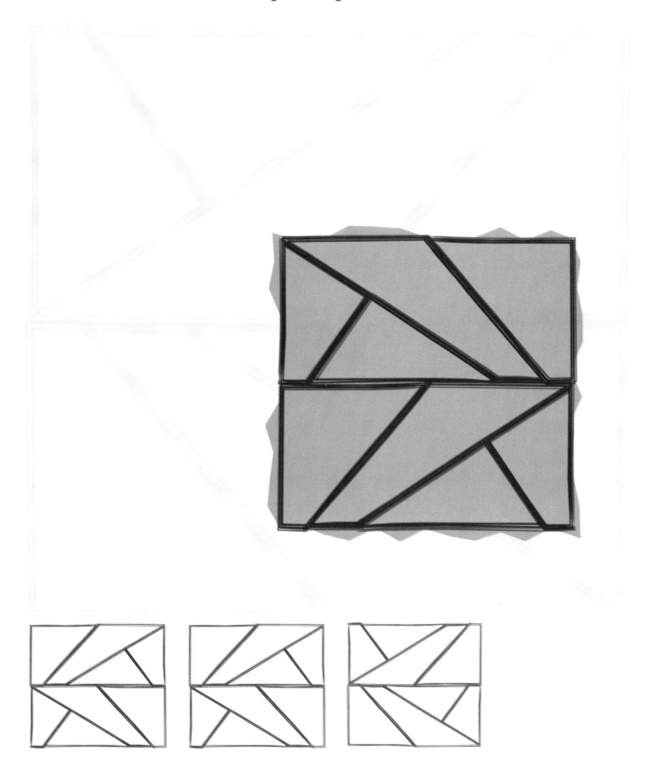

A New Spin Yardages

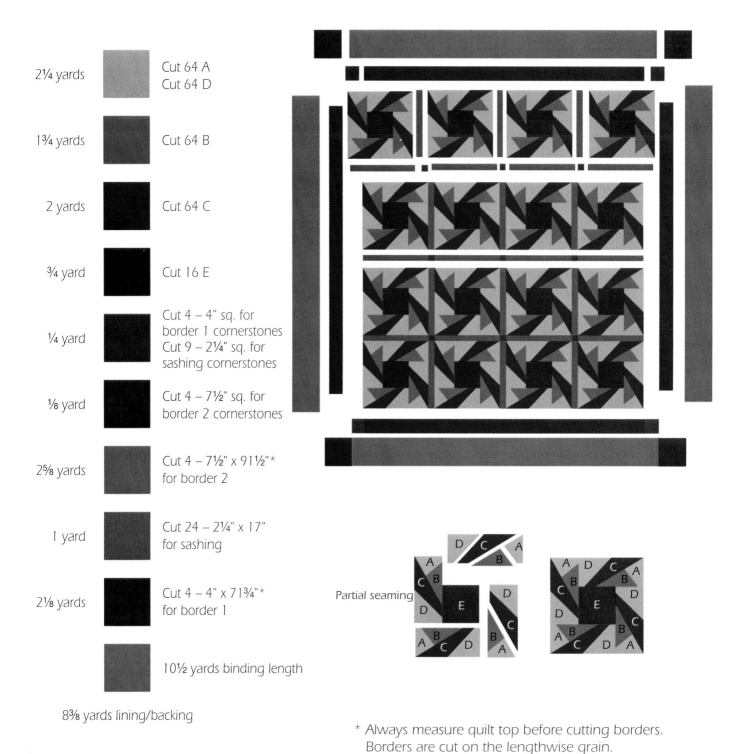

2¼ yards — Cut 64 A / Cut 64 D

1¾ yards — Cut 64 B

2 yards — Cut 64 C

¾ yard — Cut 16 E

¼ yard — Cut 4 – 4" sq. for border 1 cornerstones / Cut 9 – 2¼" sq. for sashing cornerstones

⅛ yard — Cut 4 – 7½" sq. for border 2 cornerstones

2⅝ yards — Cut 4 – 7½" x 91½"* for border 2

1 yard — Cut 24 – 2¼" x 17" for sashing

2⅛ yards — Cut 4 – 4" x 71¾"* for border 1

10½ yards binding length

8⅜ yards lining/backing

Partial seaming

* Always measure quilt top before cutting borders.
  Borders are cut on the lengthwise grain.

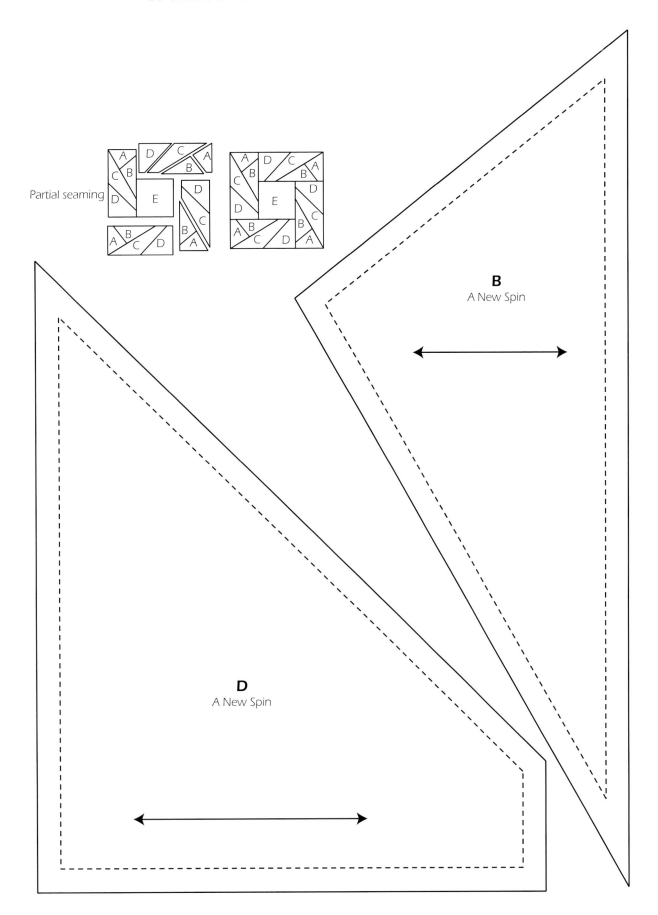

Partial seaming

B
A New Spin

D
A New Spin

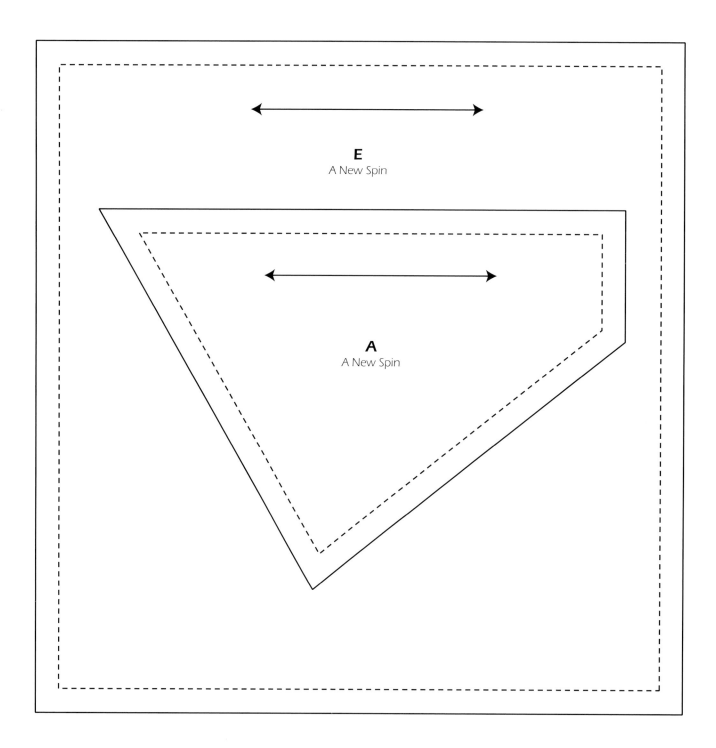

E
A New Spin

A
A New Spin

Taking Flight block patterns

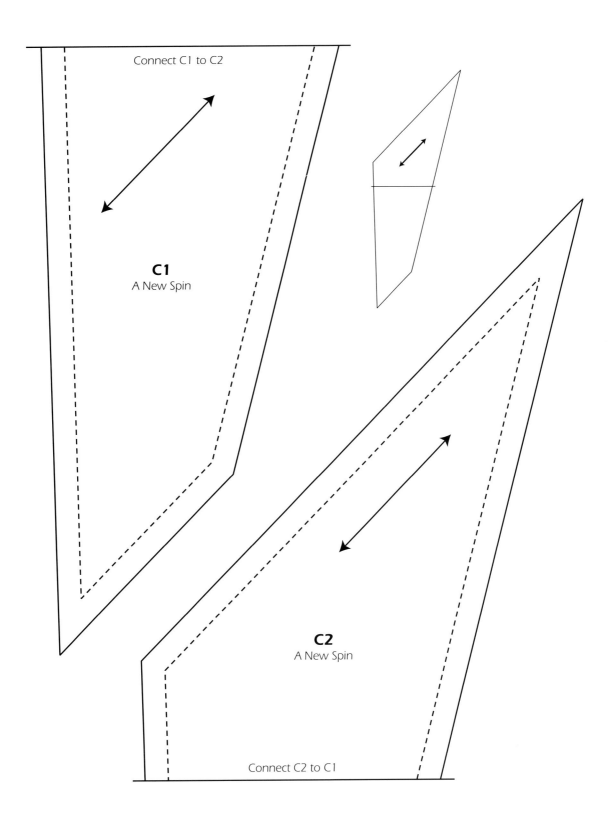

Connect C1 to C2

C1
A New Spin

C2
A New Spin

Connect C2 to C1

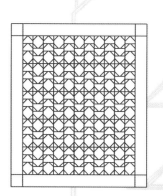

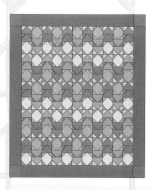

Hearts In The Garden

Use Cut Glass block.

Patterns on pages 47–49

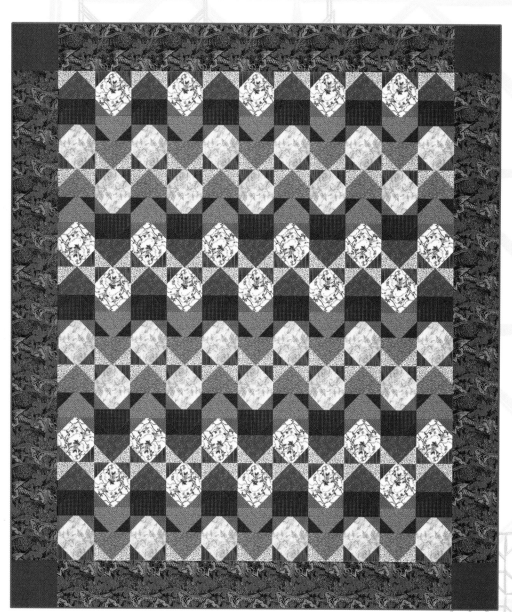

80" x 93" finished size
6" wide strip
7" border

New Classic Quilt Designs – Michal Mussell

Cut Glass block

HEARTS IN THE GARDEN YARDAGES

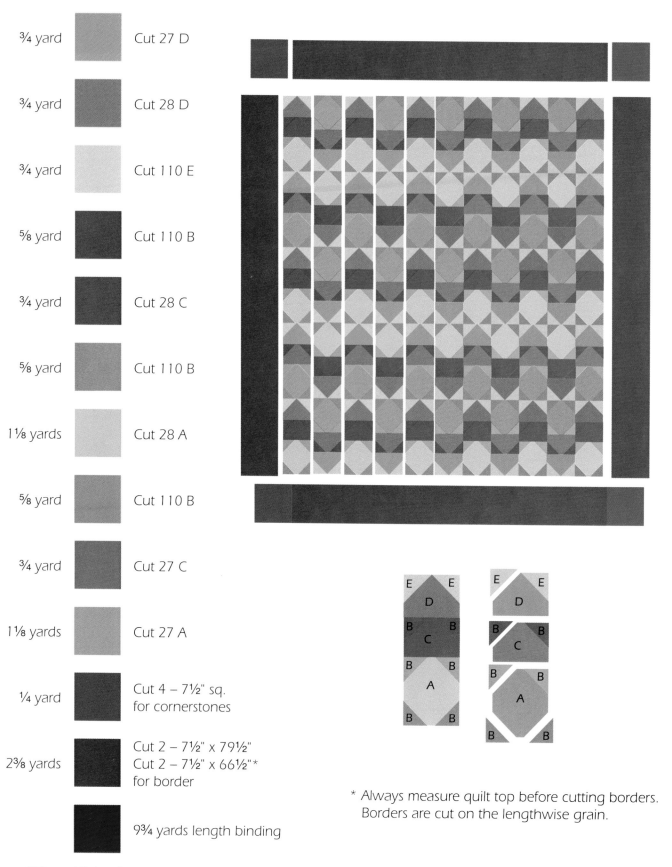

¾ yard — Cut 27 D

¾ yard — Cut 28 D

¾ yard — Cut 110 E

⅝ yard — Cut 110 B

¾ yard — Cut 28 C

⅝ yard — Cut 110 B

1⅛ yards — Cut 28 A

⅝ yard — Cut 110 B

¾ yard — Cut 27 C

1⅛ yards — Cut 27 A

¼ yard — Cut 4 – 7½" sq.
for cornerstones

2⅜ yards — Cut 2 – 7½" x 79½"
Cut 2 – 7½" x 66½"*
for border

9¾ yards length binding

5¾ yard lining/backing

* Always measure quilt top before cutting borders.
Borders are cut on the lengthwise grain.

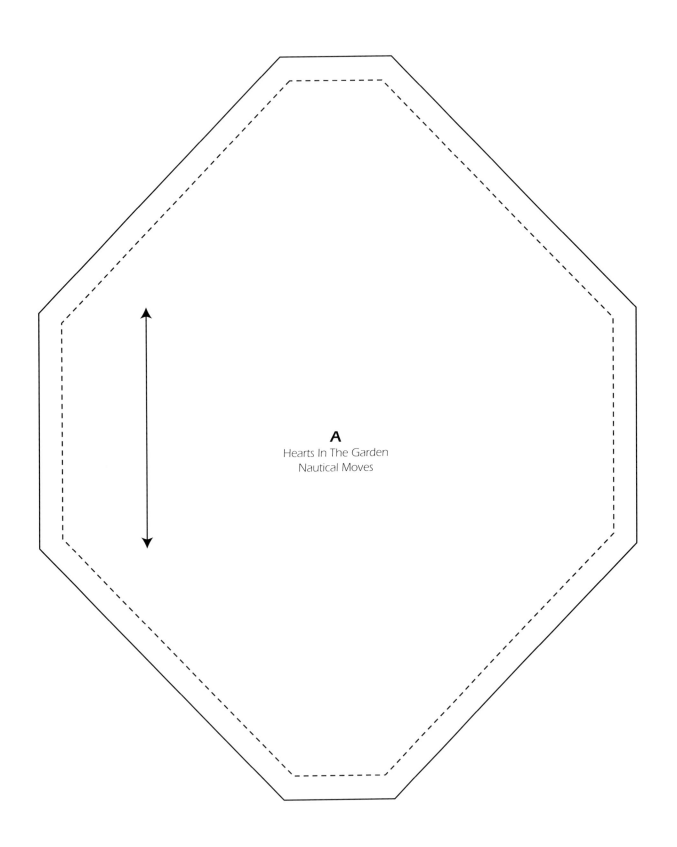

A
Hearts In The Garden
Nautical Moves

CUT GLASS BLOCK PATTERNS

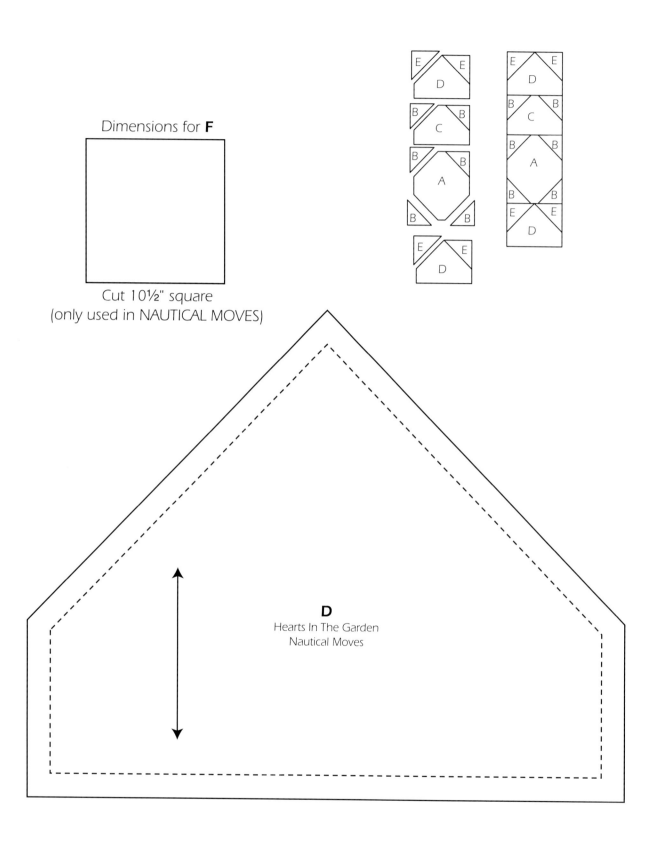

Dimensions for **F**

Cut 10½" square
(only used in NAUTICAL MOVES)

D
Hearts In The Garden
Nautical Moves

Cut Glass block patterns

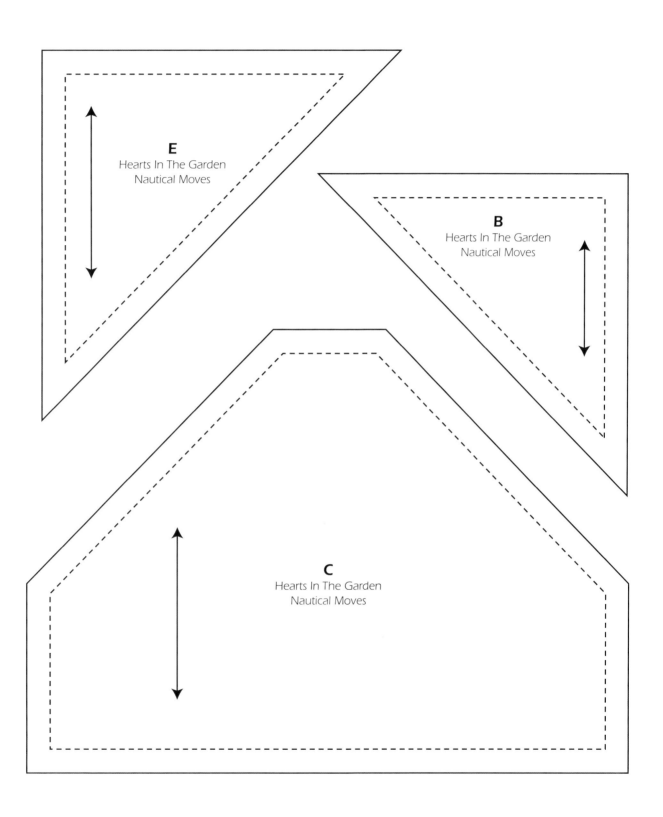

E
Hearts In The Garden
Nautical Moves

B
Hearts In The Garden
Nautical Moves

C
Hearts In The Garden
Nautical Moves

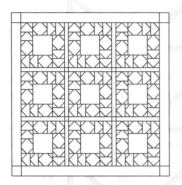

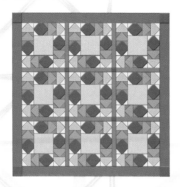

NAUTICAL MOVES

Use Cut Glass block.
Patterns on pages 47–49

80" x 80" finished size
22" block
2" sashing
5" borders

New Classic Quilt Designs – Michal Mussell

NAUTICAL MOVES YARDAGES

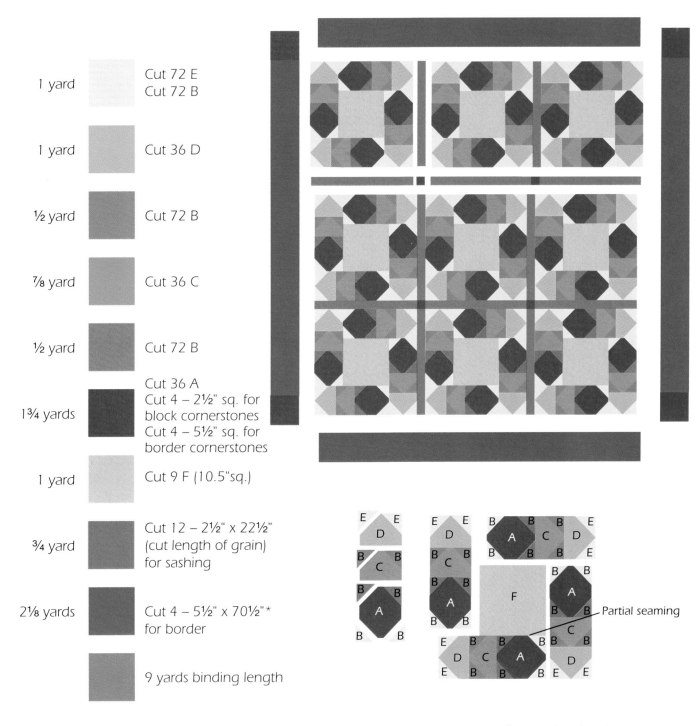

1 yard — Cut 72 E / Cut 72 B

1 yard — Cut 36 D

½ yard — Cut 72 B

⅞ yard — Cut 36 C

½ yard — Cut 72 B

1¾ yards — Cut 36 A / Cut 4 – 2½" sq. for block cornerstones / Cut 4 – 5½" sq. for border cornerstones

1 yard — Cut 9 F (10.5"sq.)

¾ yard — Cut 12 – 2½" x 22½" (cut length of grain) for sashing

2⅛ yards — Cut 4 – 5½" x 70½"* for border

9 yards binding length

5 yards for lining/backing

* Always measure quilt top before cutting borders.
  Borders are cut on the lengthwise grain.

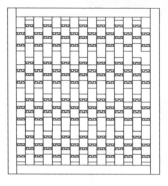

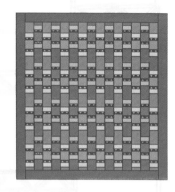

OWLS IN PARADISE

Use Boxes of Thorns block.

Patterns on pages 55–57

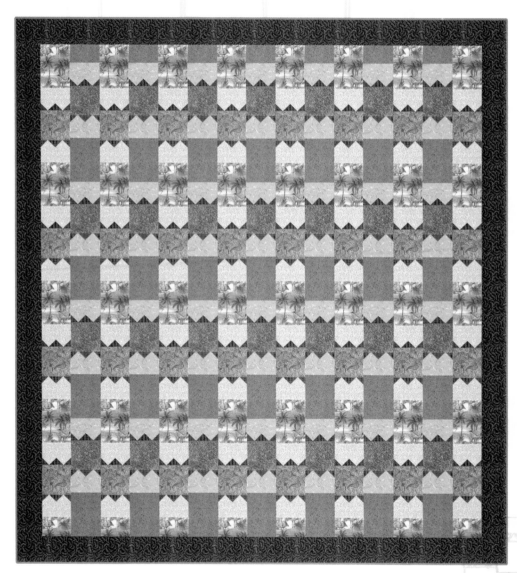

102" x 108" finished size
6" border

New Classic Quilt Designs – Michal Mussell

Boxes of Thorns block

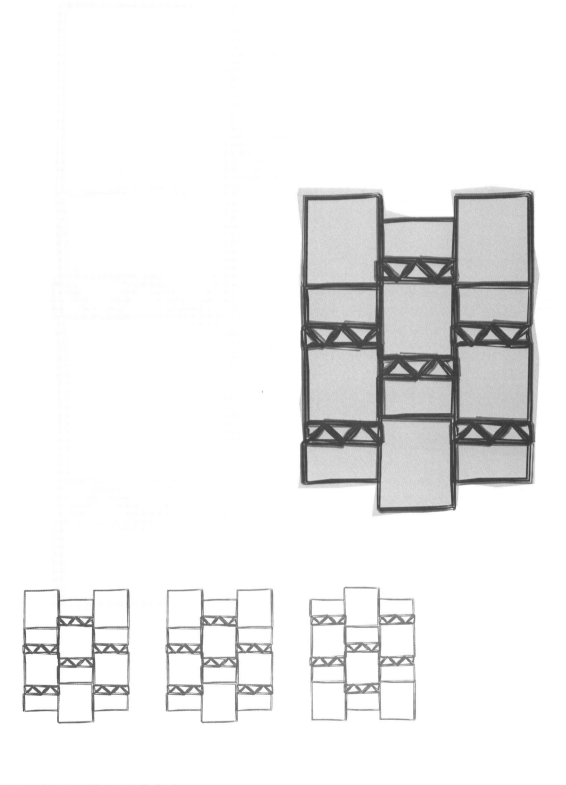

OWLS IN PARADISE YARDAGES

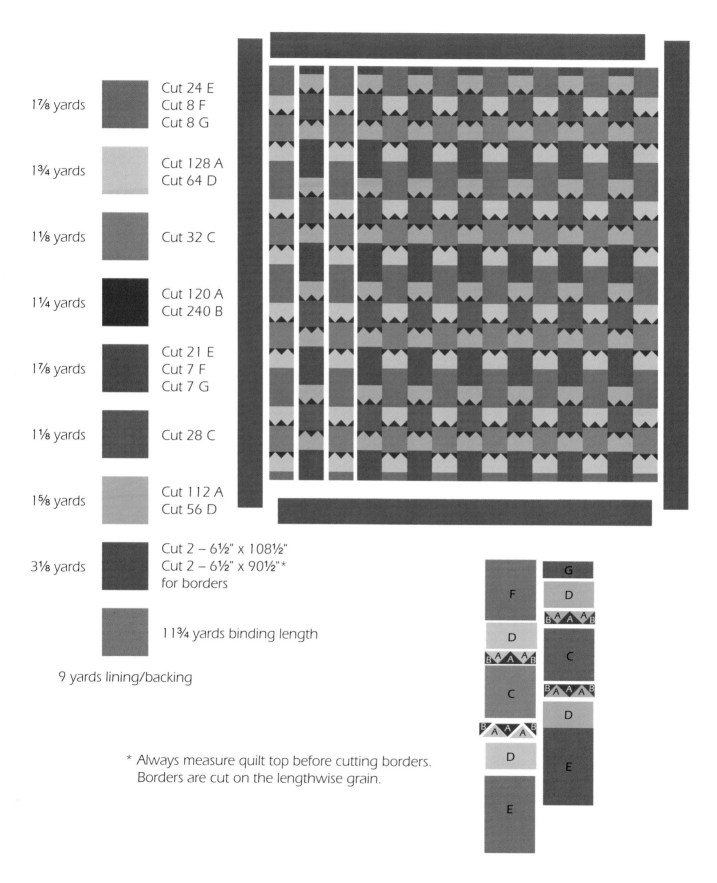

1⅞ yards — Cut 24 E / Cut 8 F / Cut 8 G

1¾ yards — Cut 128 A / Cut 64 D

1⅛ yards — Cut 32 C

1¼ yards — Cut 120 A / Cut 240 B

1⅞ yards — Cut 21 E / Cut 7 F / Cut 7 G

1⅛ yards — Cut 28 C

1⅝ yards — Cut 112 A / Cut 56 D

3⅛ yards — Cut 2 – 6½" x 108½" / Cut 2 – 6½" x 90½"* / for borders

11¾ yards binding length

9 yards lining/backing

* Always measure quilt top before cutting borders.
Borders are cut on the lengthwise grain.

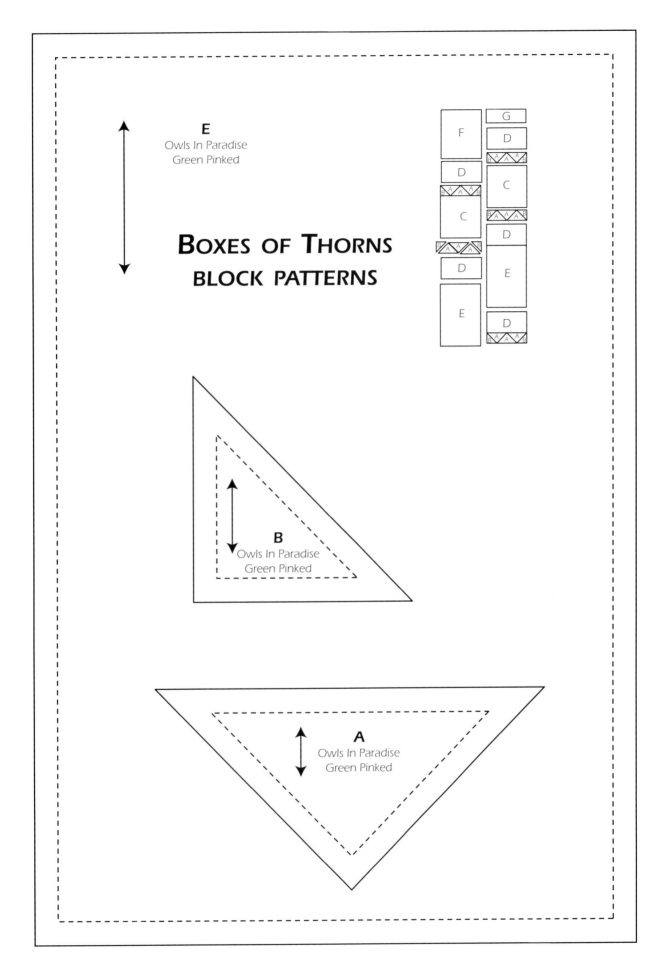

BOXES OF THORNS
BLOCK PATTERNS

E
Owls In Paradise
Green Pinked

B
Owls In Paradise
Green Pinked

A
Owls In Paradise
Green Pinked

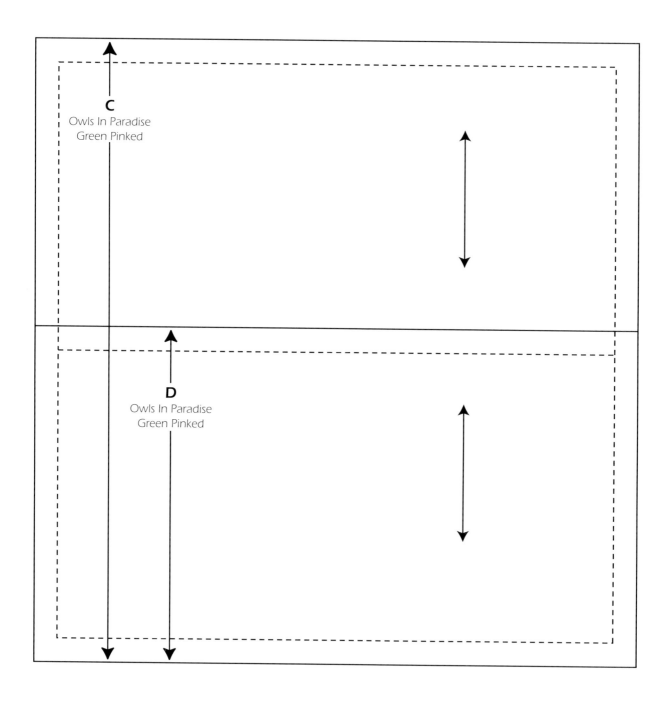

C
Owls In Paradise
Green Pinked

D
Owls In Paradise
Green Pinked

BOXES OF THORNS BLOCK PATTERNS

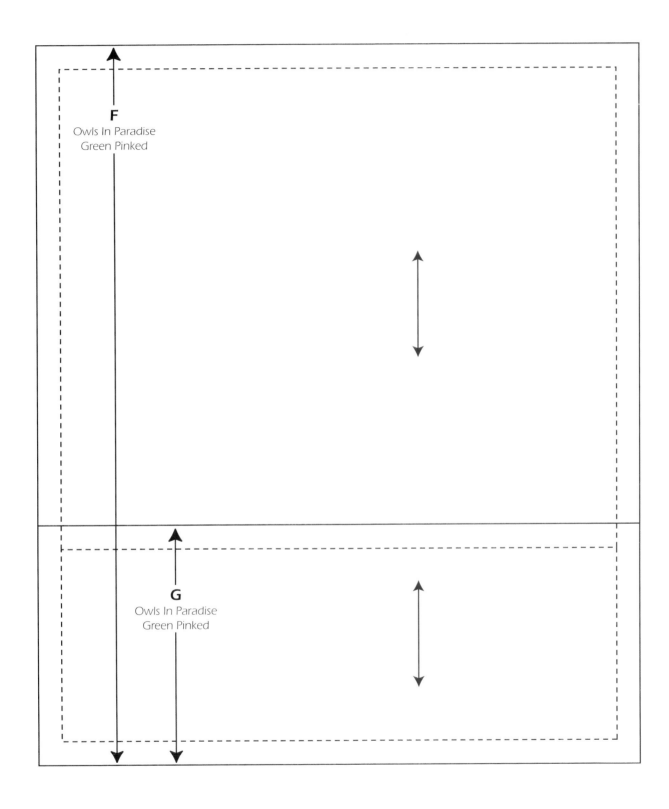

F
Owls In Paradise
Green Pinked

G
Owls In Paradise
Green Pinked

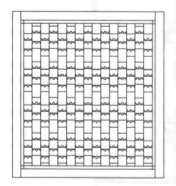
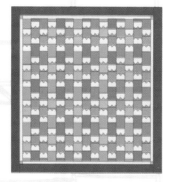

GREEN PINKED

Use Boxes of Thorns block.

Patterns on pages 55–57

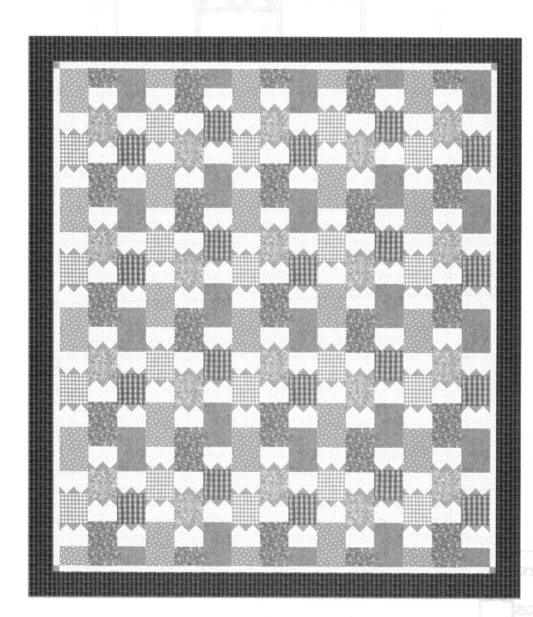

106" x 112" finished size
2" & 6" borders

GREEN PINKED YARDAGES

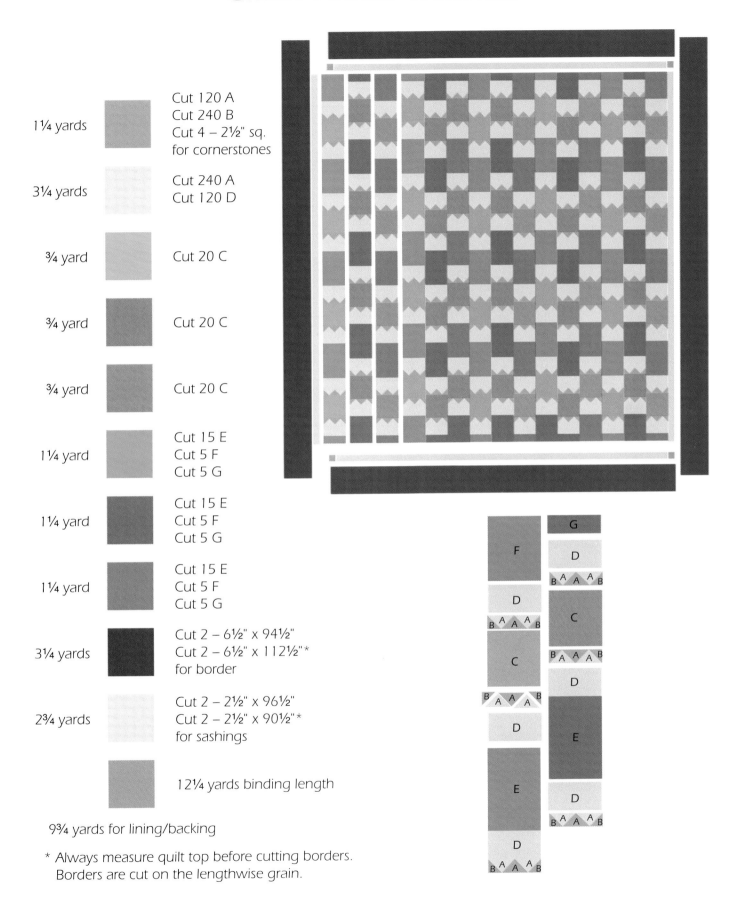

1¼ yards — Cut 120 A
Cut 240 B
Cut 4 – 2½" sq.
for cornerstones

3¼ yards — Cut 240 A
Cut 120 D

¾ yard — Cut 20 C

¾ yard — Cut 20 C

¾ yard — Cut 20 C

1¼ yard — Cut 15 E
Cut 5 F
Cut 5 G

1¼ yard — Cut 15 E
Cut 5 F
Cut 5 G

1¼ yard — Cut 15 E
Cut 5 F
Cut 5 G

3¼ yards — Cut 2 – 6½" x 94½"
Cut 2 – 6½" x 112½"*
for border

2¾ yards — Cut 2 – 2½" x 96½"
Cut 2 – 2½" x 90½"*
for sashings

12¼ yards binding length

9¾ yards for lining/backing

* Always measure quilt top before cutting borders.
  Borders are cut on the lengthwise grain.

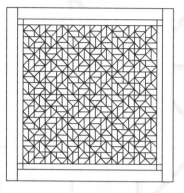

BURGUNDY BREW

Use Several Pieces block.
Patterns on page 63

105" x 105" finished size
14" block
3½" & 7" borders

Several Pieces block

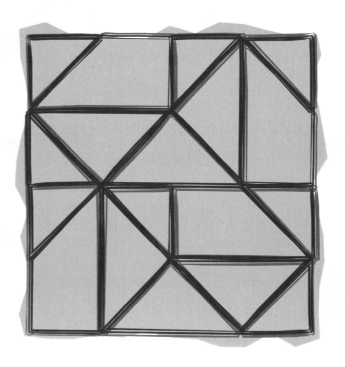

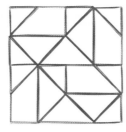 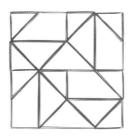 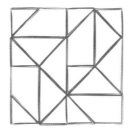

Burgundy Brew Yardages

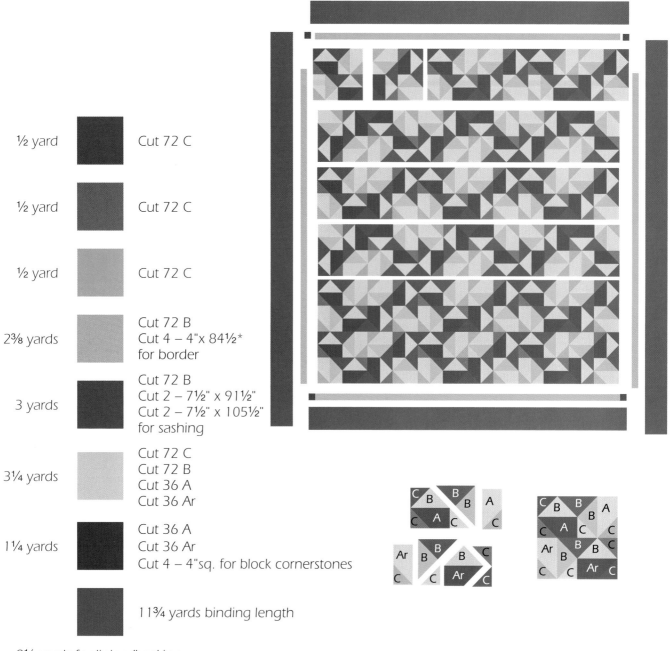

½ yard   Cut 72 C

½ yard   Cut 72 C

½ yard   Cut 72 C

2⅜ yards   Cut 72 B
Cut 4 – 4"x 84½"*
for border

3 yards   Cut 72 B
Cut 2 – 7½" x 91½"
Cut 2 – 7½" x 105½"
for sashing

3¼ yards   Cut 72 C
Cut 72 B
Cut 36 A
Cut 36 Ar

1¼ yards   Cut 36 A
Cut 36 Ar
Cut 4 – 4"sq. for block cornerstones

11¾ yards binding length

9½ yards for lining/backing

* Always measure quilt top before cutting borders.
Borders are cut on the lengthwise grain.

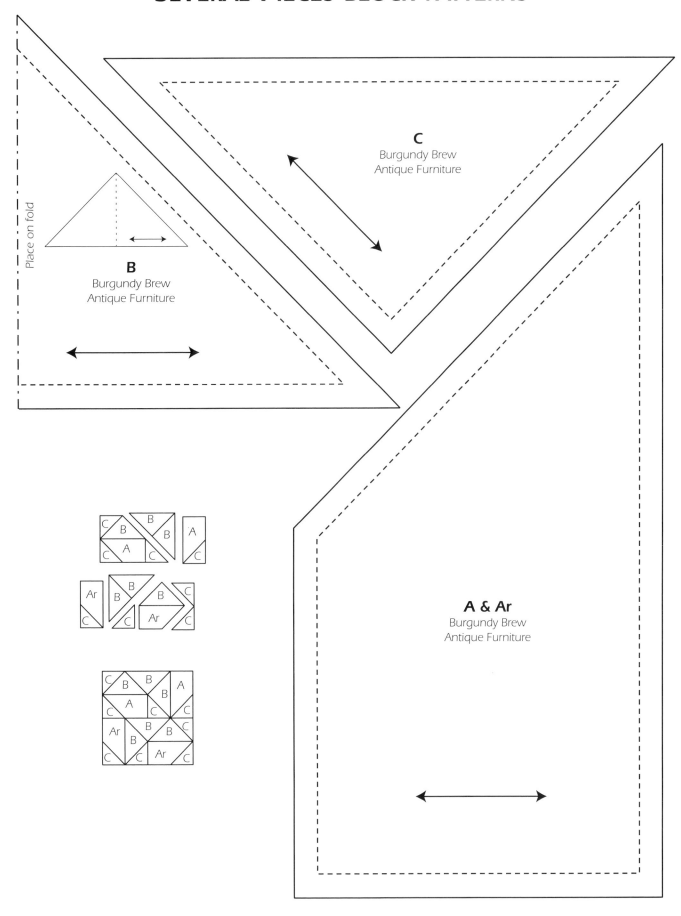

Place on fold

C
Burgundy Brew
Antique Furniture

B
Burgundy Brew
Antique Furniture

A & Ar
Burgundy Brew
Antique Furniture

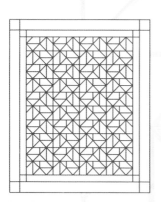
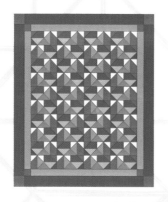

ANTIQUE FURNITURE

Use Several Pieces block.

Patterns on page 63

75" x 89" finished size
14" block
3½" & 5½" borders

New Classic Quilt Designs – Michal Mussell

ANTIQUE FURNITURE YARDAGES

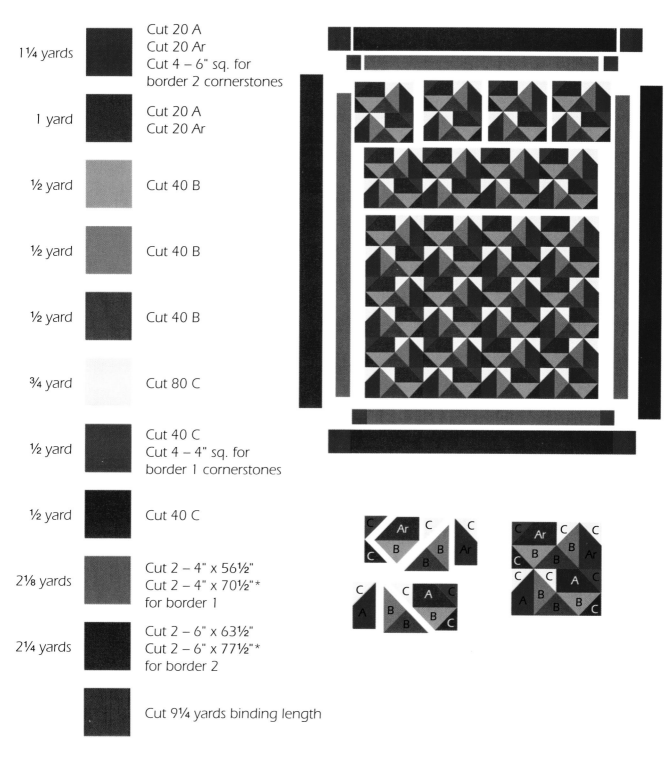

1¼ yards — Cut 20 A
Cut 20 Ar
Cut 4 – 6" sq. for
border 2 cornerstones

1 yard — Cut 20 A
Cut 20 Ar

½ yard — Cut 40 B

½ yard — Cut 40 B

½ yard — Cut 40 B

¾ yard — Cut 80 C

½ yard — Cut 40 C
Cut 4 – 4" sq. for
border 1 cornerstones

½ yard — Cut 40 C

2⅛ yards — Cut 2 – 4" x 56½"
Cut 2 – 4" x 70½"*
for border 1

2¼ yards — Cut 2 – 6" x 63½"
Cut 2 – 6" x 77½"*
for border 2

Cut 9¼ yards binding length

5¼ yards lining/backing

* Always measure quilt top before cutting borders.
Borders are cut on the lengthwise grain.

Michal Mussell – New Classic Quilt Designs

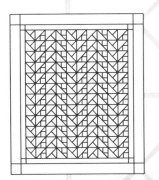
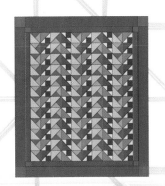

MIGRATION

Use 12" Paper Hats block.
Patterns on page 69

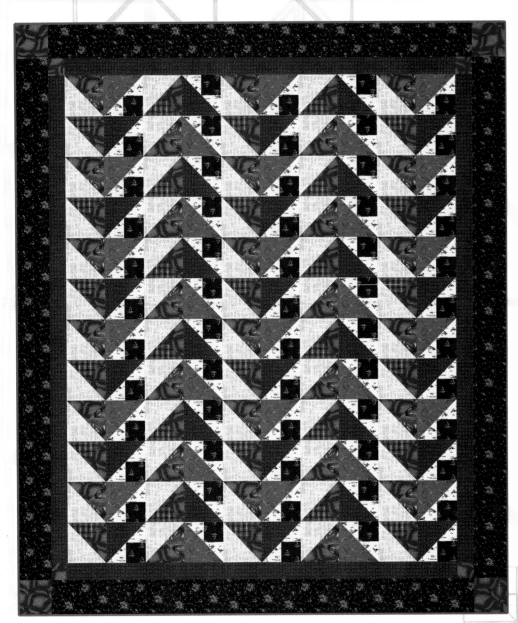

78" x 90" finished size
12" block
3" & 6" border

New Classic Quilt Designs – Michal Mussell

Paper Hats block

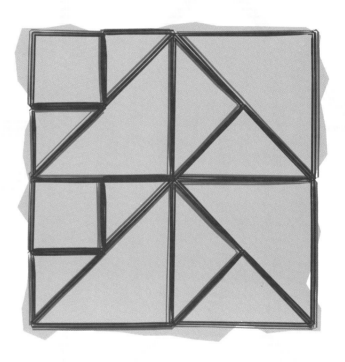

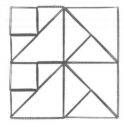 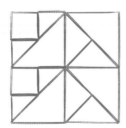 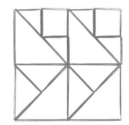

MIGRATION YARDAGES

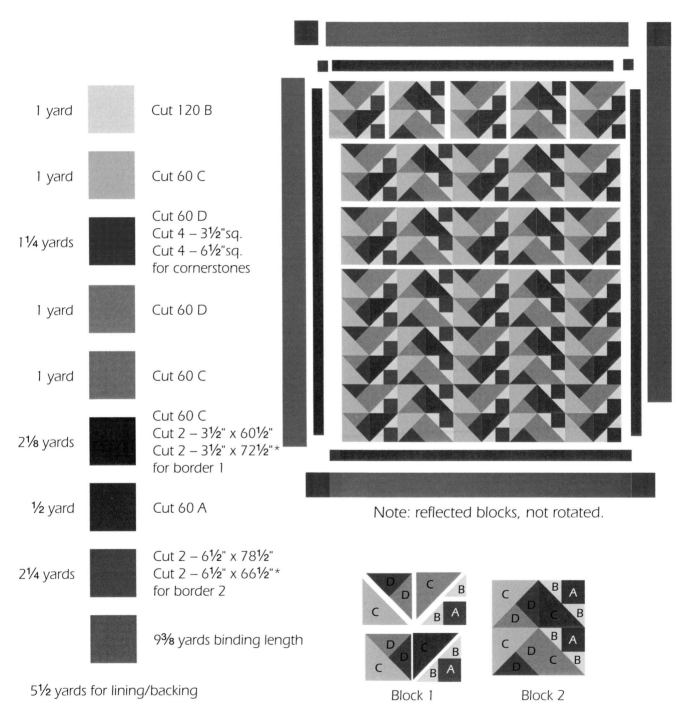

1 yard — Cut 120 B

1 yard — Cut 60 C

1¼ yards — Cut 60 D
Cut 4 – 3½"sq.
Cut 4 – 6½"sq.
for cornerstones

1 yard — Cut 60 D

1 yard — Cut 60 C

2⅛ yards — Cut 60 C
Cut 2 – 3½" x 60½"
Cut 2 – 3½" x 72½"*
for border 1

½ yard — Cut 60 A

2¼ yards — Cut 2 – 6½" x 78½"
Cut 2 – 6½" x 66½"*
for border 2

9⅜ yards binding length

5½ yards for lining/backing

Note: reflected blocks, not rotated.

Block 1   Block 2

* Always measure quilt top before cutting borders.
Borders are cut on the lengthwise grain.

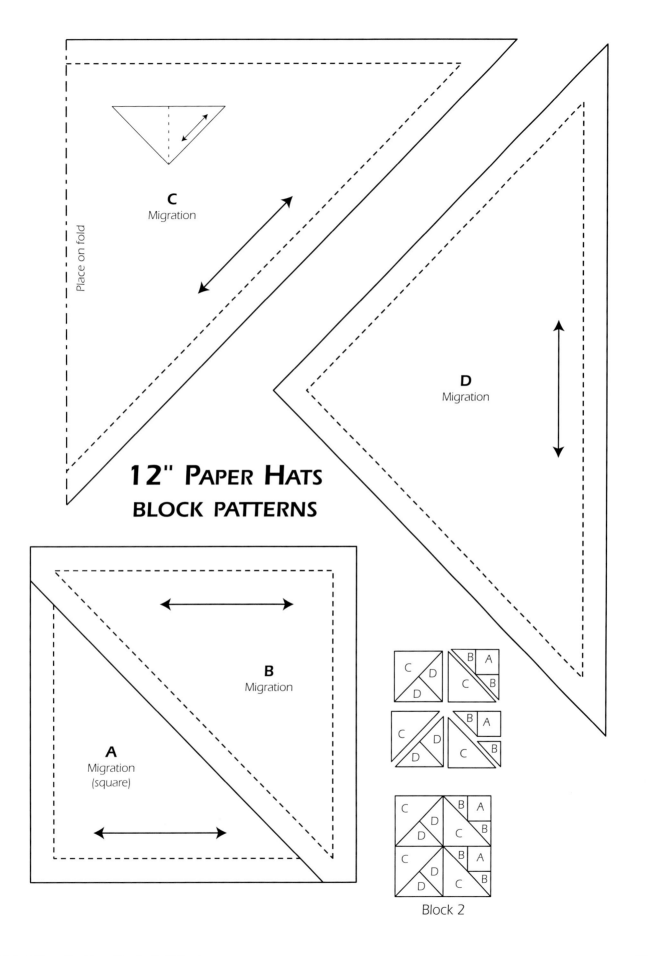

C
Migration

Place on fold

D
Migration

12" Paper Hats
Block Patterns

B
Migration

A
Migration
(square)

Block 2

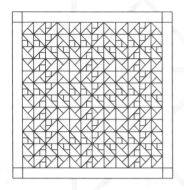

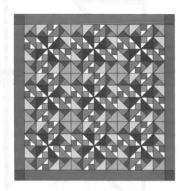

HARVEST TWIRL

Use 14" Paper Hats block.
Patterns on pages 72–73

96" x 96" finished size
14" block
6" border

New Classic Quilt Designs – Michal Mussell

Harvest Twirl Yardages

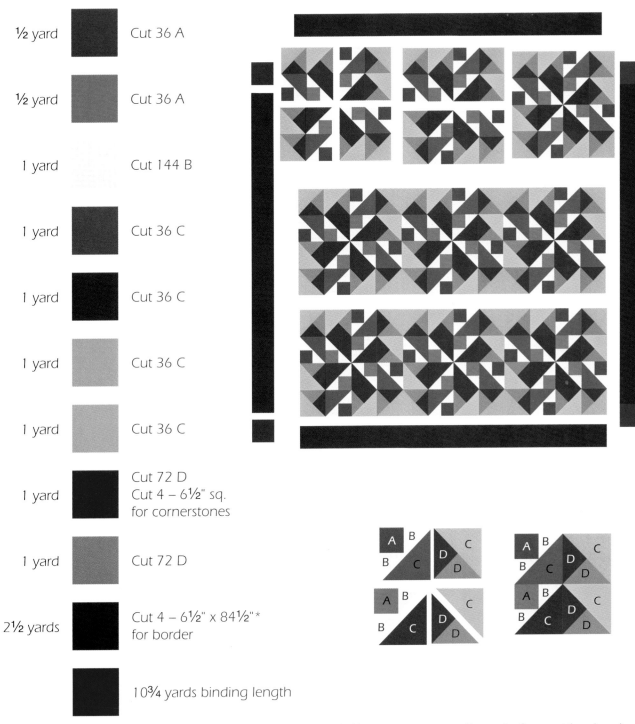

½ yard   Cut 36 A

½ yard   Cut 36 A

1 yard   Cut 144 B

1 yard   Cut 36 C

1 yard   Cut 36 C

1 yard   Cut 36 C

1 yard   Cut 36 C

1 yard   Cut 72 D
Cut 4 – 6½" sq.
for cornerstones

1 yard   Cut 72 D

2½ yards   Cut 4 – 6½" x 84½"*
for border

10¾ yards binding length

8½ yards lining/backing

* Always measure quilt top before cutting borders.
Borders are cut on the lengthwise grain.

14" PAPER HATS BLOCK PATTERNS

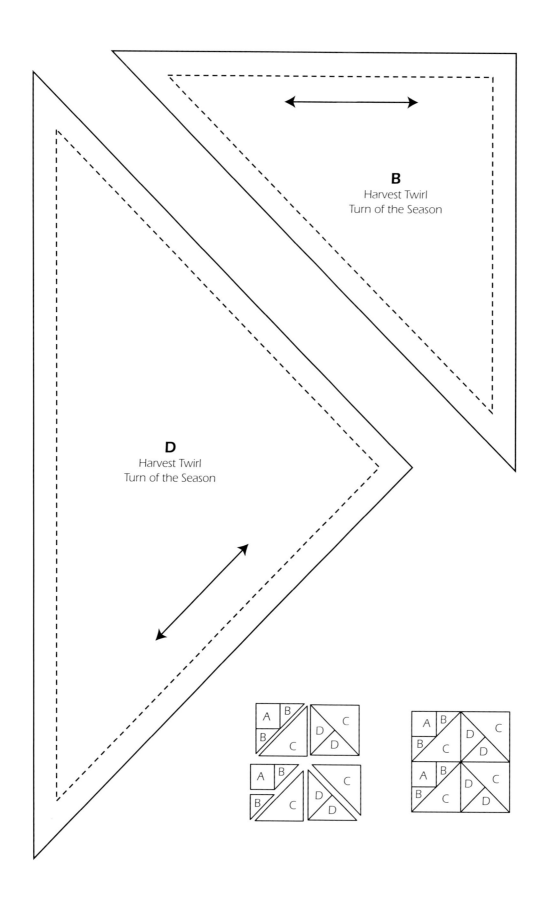

B
Harvest Twirl
Turn of the Season

D
Harvest Twirl
Turn of the Season

New Classic Quilt Designs – Michal Mussell

14" Paper Hats block patterns

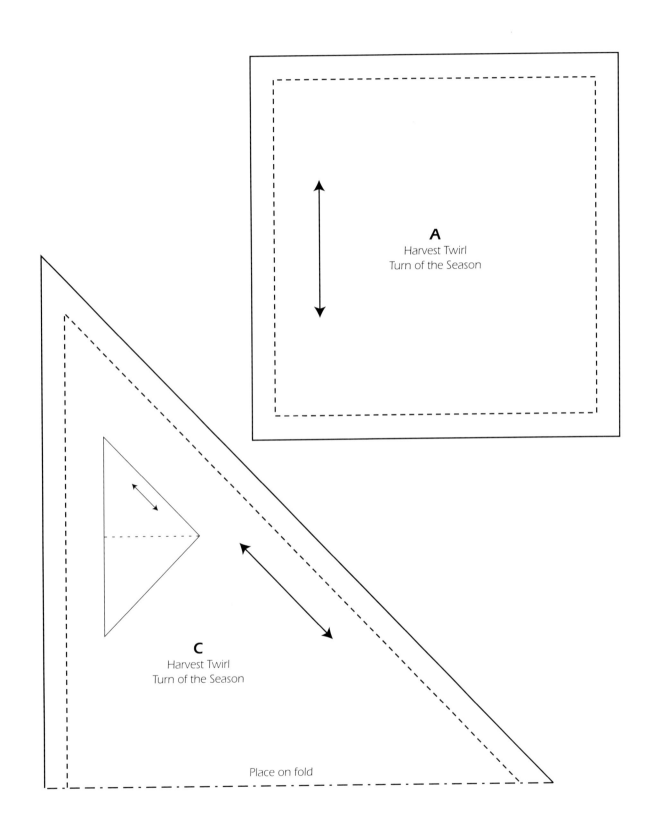

A
Harvest Twirl
Turn of the Season

C
Harvest Twirl
Turn of the Season

Place on fold

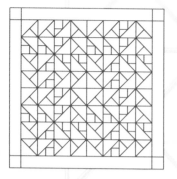

TURN OF THE SEASON

Use 14" Paper Hats block.

Patterns on pages 72–73

66" x 66" finished size
14" block
6" border

New Classic Quilt Designs – Michal Mussell

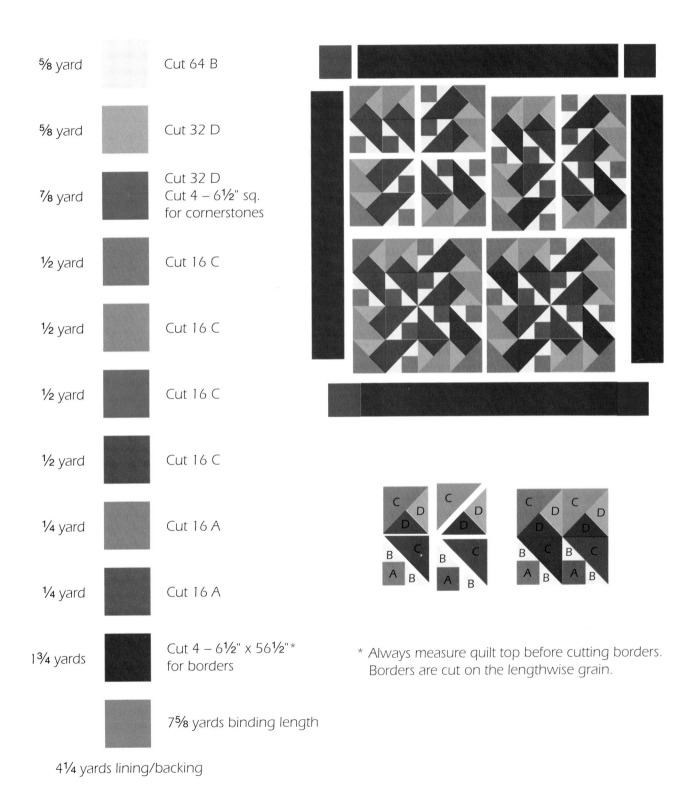

⅝ yard — Cut 64 B

⅝ yard — Cut 32 D

⅞ yard — Cut 32 D
Cut 4 – 6½" sq.
for cornerstones

½ yard — Cut 16 C

½ yard — Cut 16 C

½ yard — Cut 16 C

½ yard — Cut 16 C

¼ yard — Cut 16 A

¼ yard — Cut 16 A

1¾ yards — Cut 4 – 6½" x 56½"*
for borders

7⅝ yards binding length

4¼ yards lining/backing

* Always measure quilt top before cutting borders.
Borders are cut on the lengthwise grain.

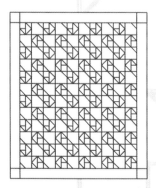
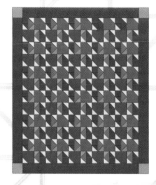

PIMENTOS IN OLIVES

Use 14" Bird's Beak block.
Patterns on pages 79–80

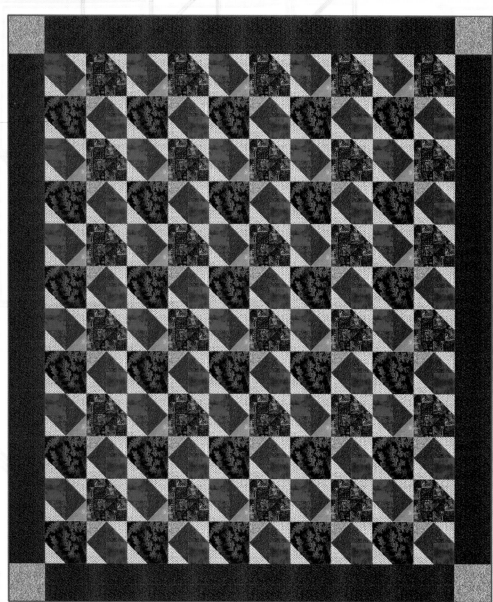

82" x 96" finished size
14" block
6" border

Bird's Beak block

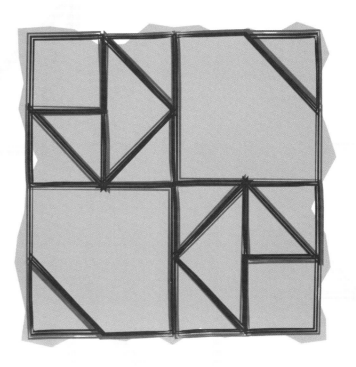

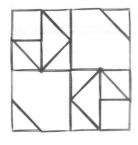
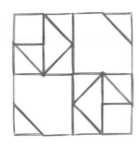
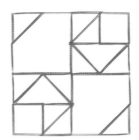

Pimentos in Olives Yardages

¾ yard — Cut 60 B

1¼ yards — Cut 180 A

½ yard — Cut 60 A

⅞ yard — Cut 60 C

¼ yard — Cut 30 A

½ yard — Cut 30 A
Cut 4 – 6½" sq.
for cornerstones

1½ yards — Cut 30 D

1½ yards — Cut 30 D

2 yards — Cut 2 – 6½" x 70½"
Cut 2 – 6½" x 48½"*
for borders

10 yards binding length

6 yards for lining/backing

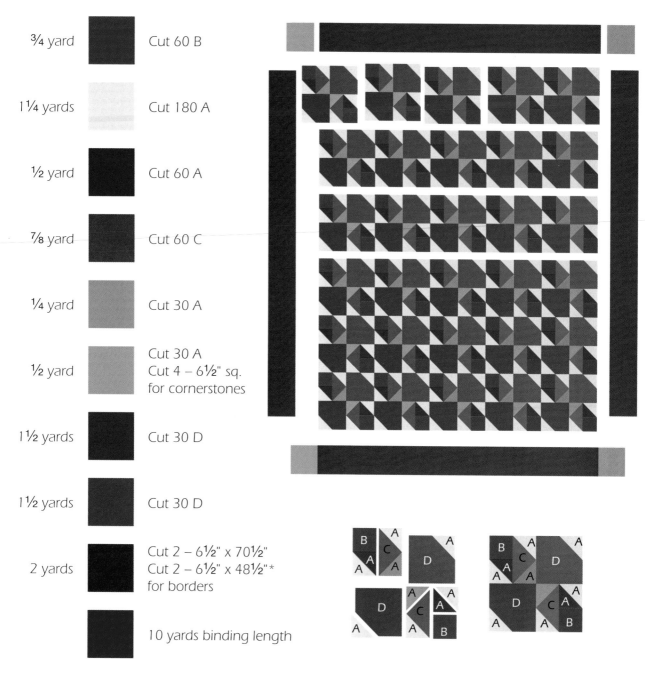

* Always measure quilt top before cutting borders.
Borders are cut on the lengthwise grain.

New Classic Quilt Designs – Michal Mussell

14" Bird's Beak block patterns

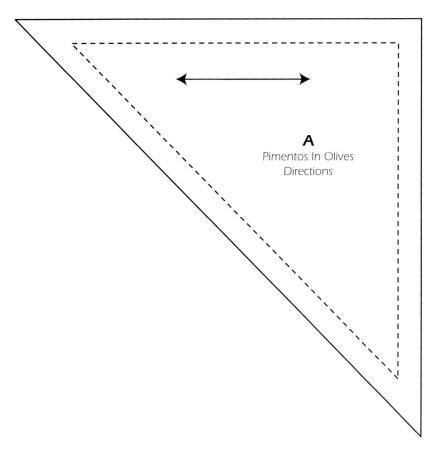

A
Pimentos In Olives
Directions

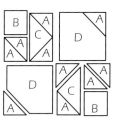

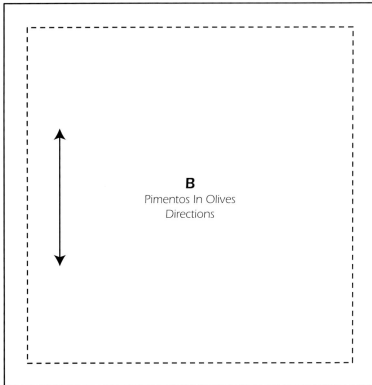

B
Pimentos In Olives
Directions

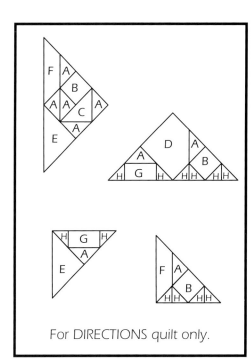

For DIRECTIONS quilt only.

14" BIRD'S BEAK BLOCK PATTERNS

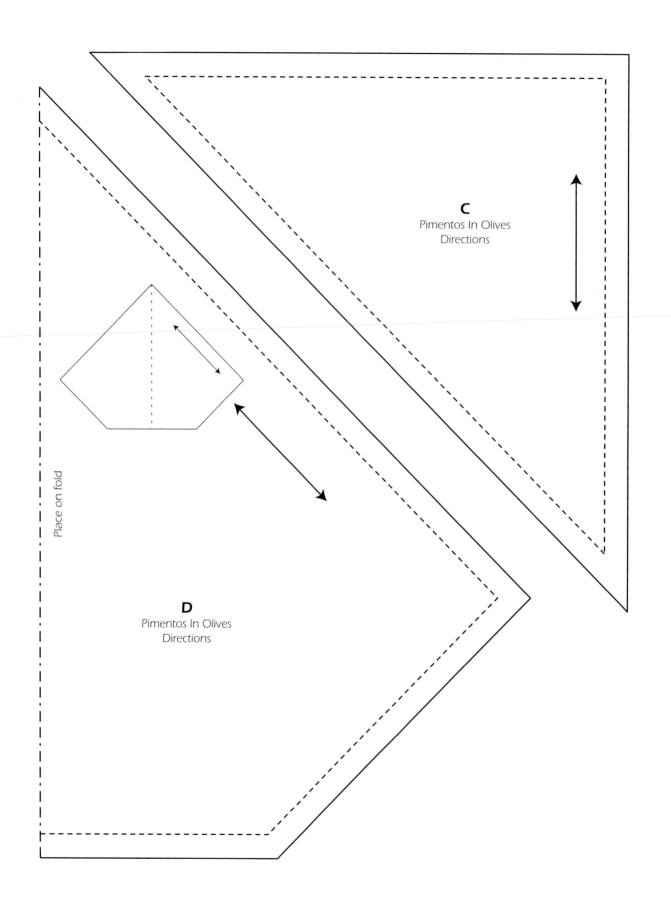

C
Pimentos In Olives
Directions

Place on fold

D
Pimentos In Olives
Directions

14" Bird's Beak block patterns

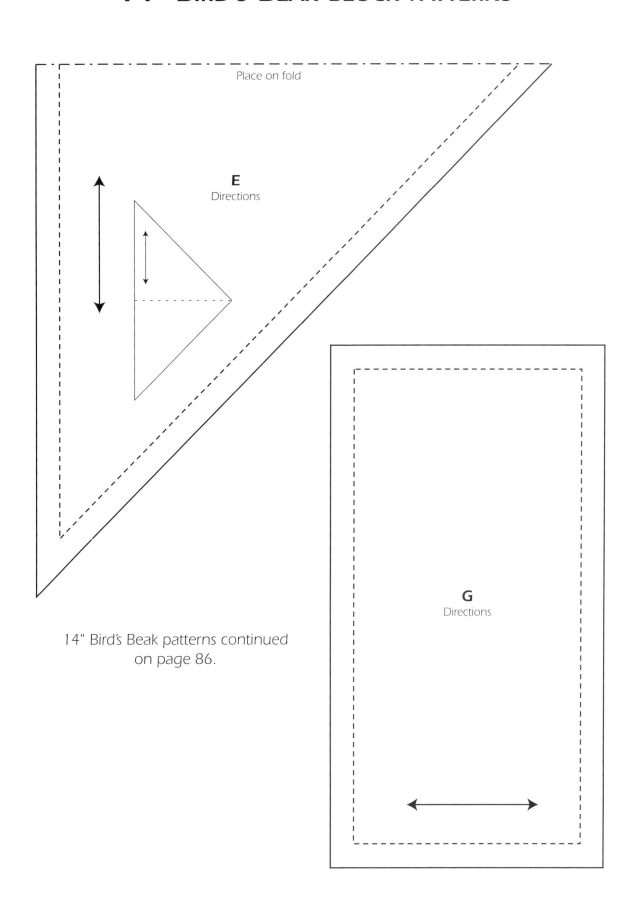

Place on fold

E
Directions

G
Directions

14" Bird's Beak patterns continued on page 86.

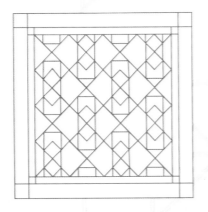

DIRECTIONS

Use 14" Bird's Beak block.

Patterns on pages 79–81, 86

52" x 52" finished size
14" block
2" & 4" borders

DIRECTIONS YARDAGES

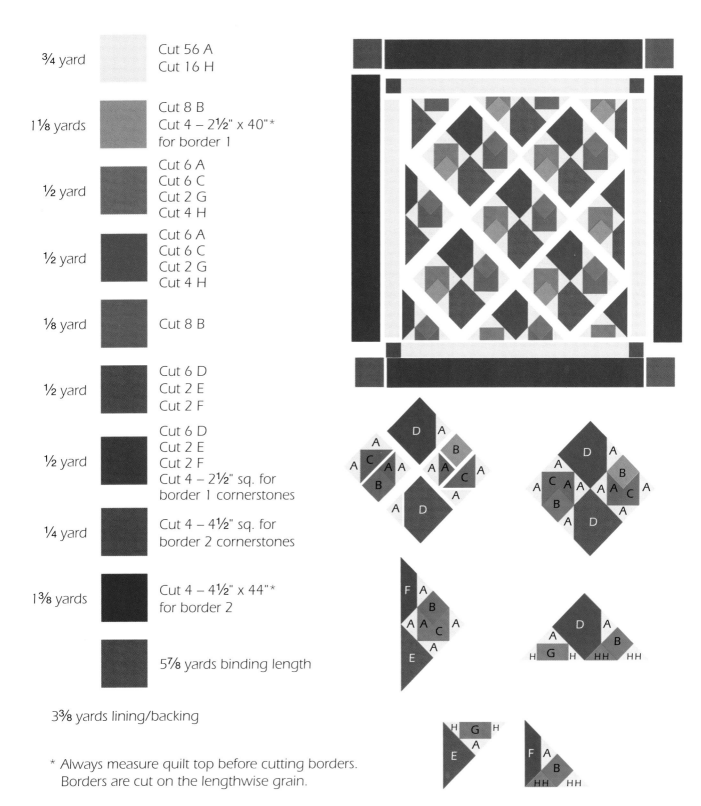

¾ yard — Cut 56 A / Cut 16 H

1⅛ yards — Cut 8 B / Cut 4 – 2½" x 40"* for border 1

½ yard — Cut 6 A / Cut 6 C / Cut 2 G / Cut 4 H

½ yard — Cut 6 A / Cut 6 C / Cut 2 G / Cut 4 H

⅛ yard — Cut 8 B

½ yard — Cut 6 D / Cut 2 E / Cut 2 F

½ yard — Cut 6 D / Cut 2 E / Cut 2 F / Cut 4 – 2½" sq. for border 1 cornerstones

¼ yard — Cut 4 – 4½" sq. for border 2 cornerstones

1⅜ yards — Cut 4 – 4½" x 44"* for border 2

5⅞ yards binding length

3⅜ yards lining/backing

* Always measure quilt top before cutting borders. Borders are cut on the lengthwise grain.

Make two of each corner; rotate according to colored assembly diagram.

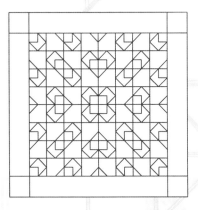

SUMMER BLOOM

Use 12" Bird's Beak block.

Patterns on pages 86–87

62" x 62" finished size
12" block
7" border

New Classic Quilt Designs – Michal Mussell

Summer Bloom Yardages

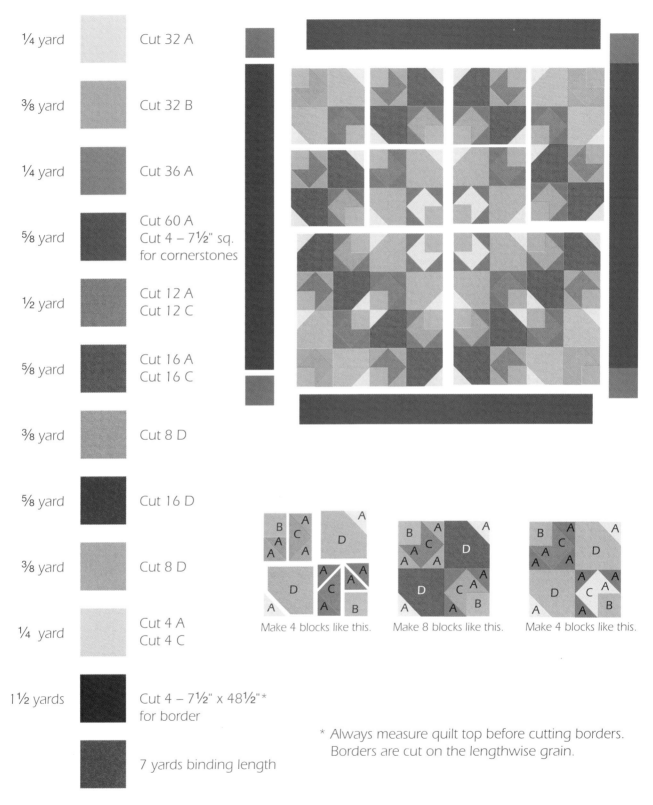

¼ yard — Cut 32 A

⅜ yard — Cut 32 B

¼ yard — Cut 36 A

⅝ yard — Cut 60 A
Cut 4 – 7½" sq.
for cornerstones

½ yard — Cut 12 A
Cut 12 C

⅝ yard — Cut 16 A
Cut 16 C

⅜ yard — Cut 8 D

⅝ yard — Cut 16 D

⅜ yard — Cut 8 D

¼ yard — Cut 4 A
Cut 4 C

1½ yards — Cut 4 – 7½" x 48½"*
for border

7 yards binding length

4 yards for lining/backing

Make 4 blocks like this.

Make 8 blocks like this.

Make 4 blocks like this.

*Always measure quilt top before cutting borders.
Borders are cut on the lengthwise grain.

12" Bird's Beak block patterns

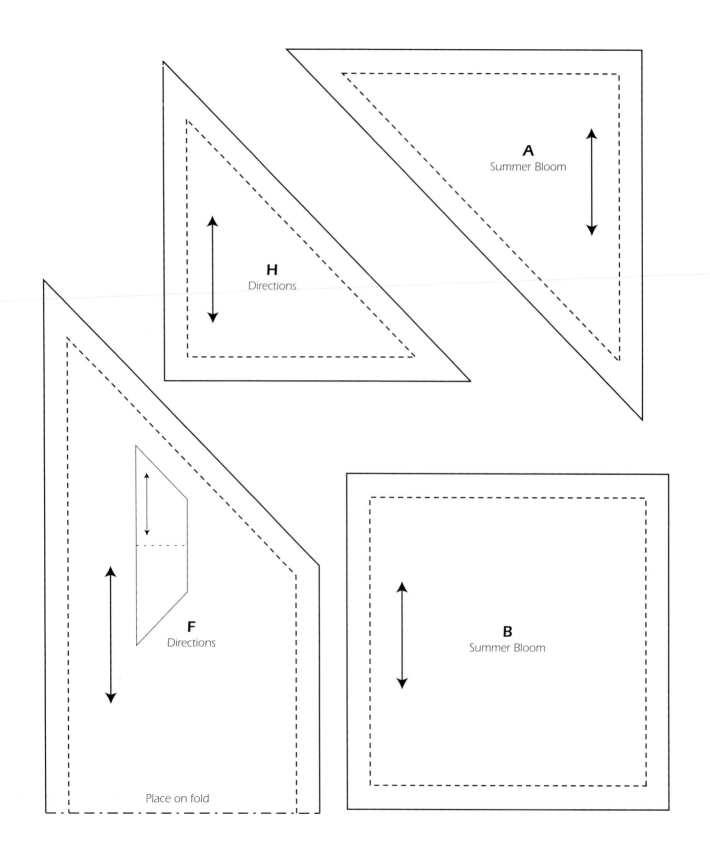

A
Summer Bloom

H
Directions

F
Directions

Place on fold

B
Summer Bloom

12" Bird's Beak block patterns

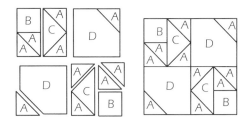

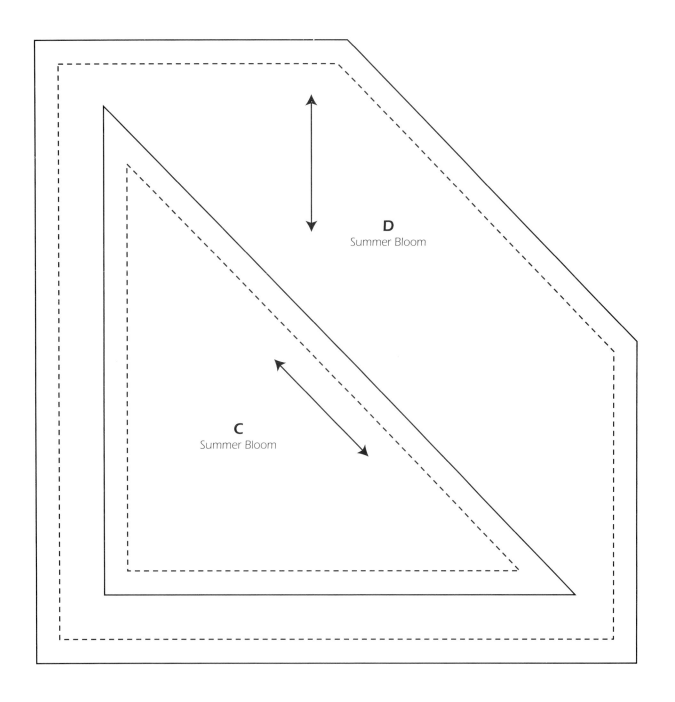

D
Summer Bloom

C
Summer Bloom

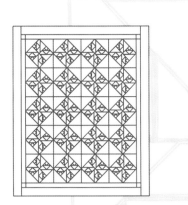
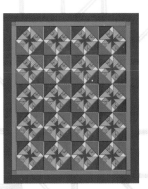

GENTLE TOUCH

Use Give It A Whirl block.

Patterns on page 91

98" x 117" finished size
14" block
3" & 6" borders

New Classic Quilt Designs – Michal Mussell

Give It A Whirl block

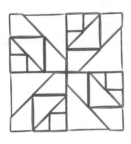 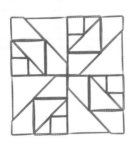 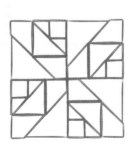

GENTLE TOUCH YARDAGES

¾ yard — Cut 80 A

¾ yard — Cut 160 B

1 yard — Cut 80 C

1 yard — Cut 80 D

¾ yard — Cut 80 Dr

1½ yards — Cut 80 E

2½ yards — Cut 20 squares for F

2½ yards — Cut 20 squares for F

⅛ yard — Cut 4 – 3½"sq. for cornerstones

2⅞ yards — Cut 2 – 3½" x 79½"
Cut 2 – 3½" x 99¼"*
for border 1

3⅜ yards — Cut 2 – 6½" x 85½"
Cut 2 – 6½" x 117¼"*
for border 2

12⅛ yards binding length

10⅛ yards lining/backing

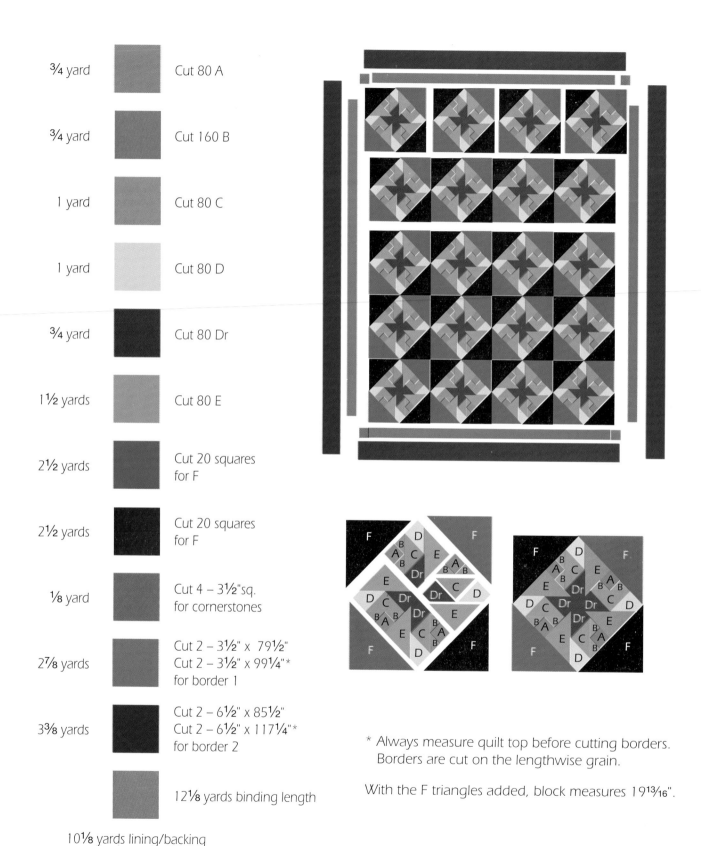

* Always measure quilt top before cutting borders.
  Borders are cut on the lengthwise grain.

With the F triangles added, block measures 19¹³⁄₁₆".

GIVE IT A WHIRL BLOCK PATTERNS

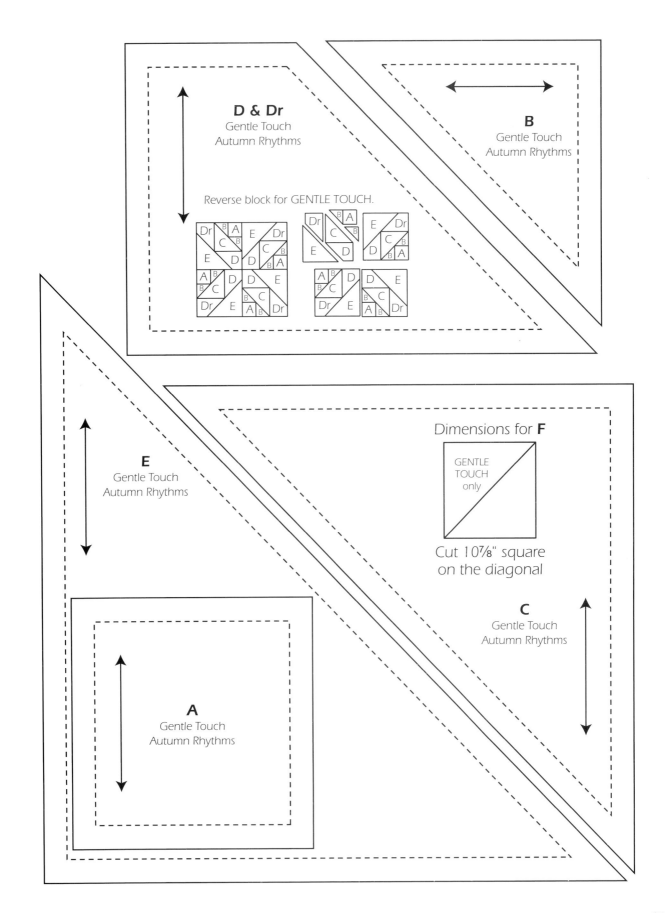

D & Dr
Gentle Touch
Autumn Rhythms

Reverse block for GENTLE TOUCH.

B
Gentle Touch
Autumn Rhythms

E
Gentle Touch
Autumn Rhythms

Dimensions for **F**

GENTLE
TOUCH
only

Cut 10⅞" square
on the diagonal

C
Gentle Touch
Autumn Rhythms

A
Gentle Touch
Autumn Rhythms

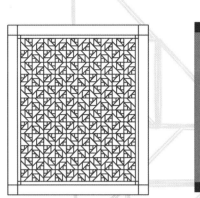
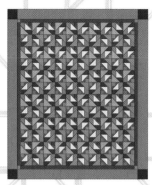

AUTUMN RHYTHMS

Use Give It A Whirl block.
Patterns on page 91

86" x 100" finished size
14" block
2" & 6" borders

New Classic Quilt Designs – Michal Mussell

Autumn Rhythms Yardages

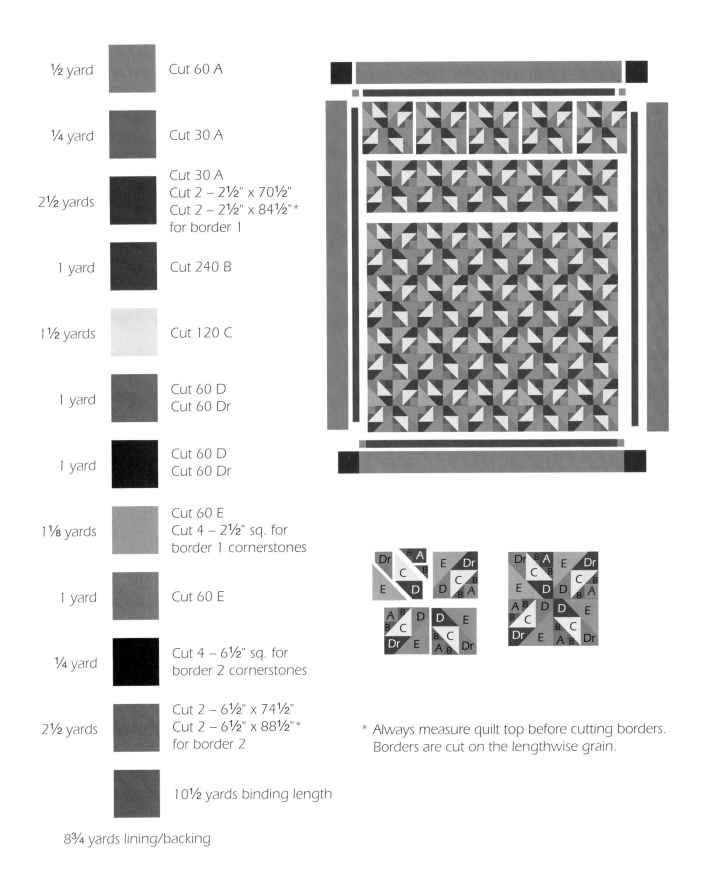

½ yard — Cut 60 A

¼ yard — Cut 30 A

2½ yards — Cut 30 A
Cut 2 – 2½" x 70½"
Cut 2 – 2½" x 84½"*
for border 1

1 yard — Cut 240 B

1½ yards — Cut 120 C

1 yard — Cut 60 D
Cut 60 Dr

1 yard — Cut 60 D
Cut 60 Dr

1⅛ yards — Cut 60 E
Cut 4 – 2½" sq. for
border 1 cornerstones

1 yard — Cut 60 E

¼ yard — Cut 4 – 6½" sq. for
border 2 cornerstones

2½ yards — Cut 2 – 6½" x 74½"
Cut 2 – 6½" x 88½"*
for border 2

10½ yards binding length

8¾ yards lining/backing

* Always measure quilt top before cutting borders.
  Borders are cut on the lengthwise grain.

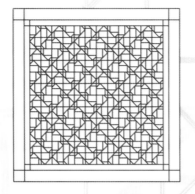
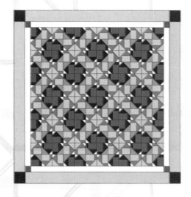

OLD PATCHES

Use 12" Zig the Zag block.

Patterns on page 97

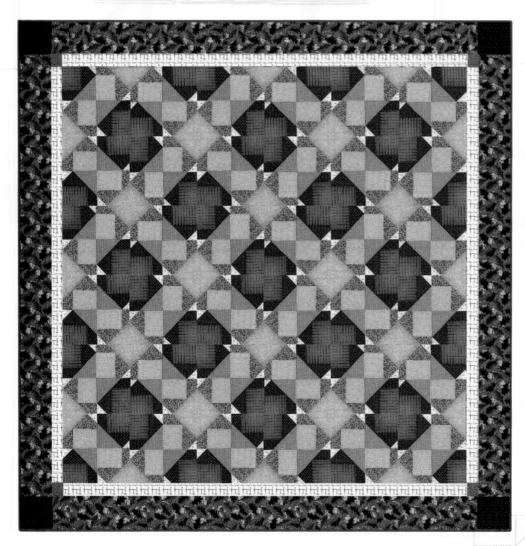

90" x 90" finished size
12" block
3" & 6" border

Zig the Zag block

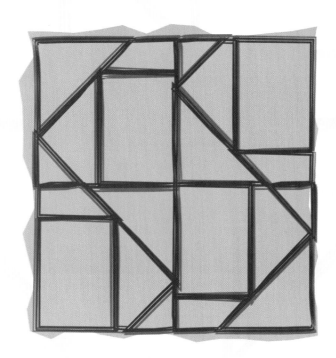

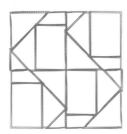 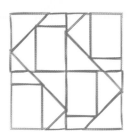 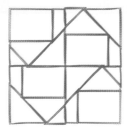

OLD PATCHES YARDAGES

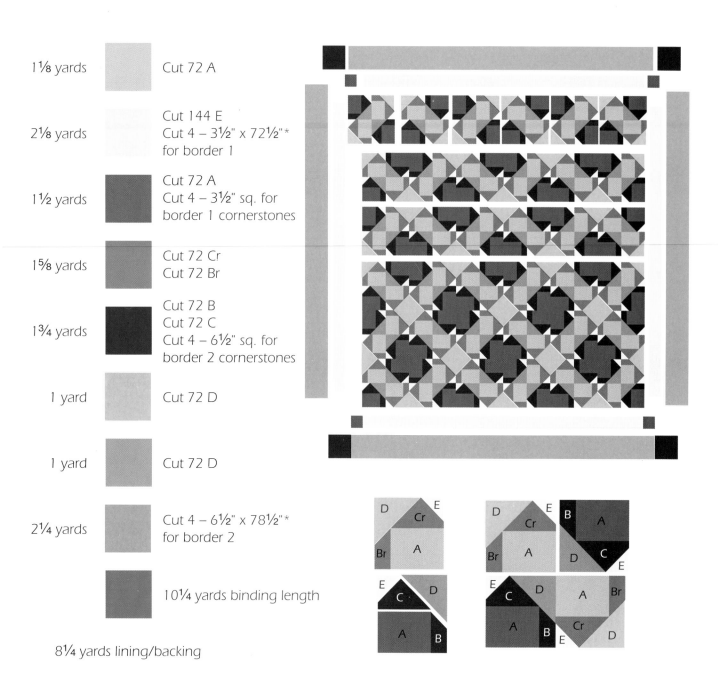

1⅛ yards — Cut 72 A

2⅛ yards — Cut 144 E
Cut 4 – 3½" x 72½"*
for border 1

1½ yards — Cut 72 A
Cut 4 – 3½" sq. for
border 1 cornerstones

1⅝ yards — Cut 72 Cr
Cut 72 Br

1¾ yards — Cut 72 B
Cut 72 C
Cut 4 – 6½" sq. for
border 2 cornerstones

1 yard — Cut 72 D

1 yard — Cut 72 D

2¼ yards — Cut 4 – 6½" x 78½"*
for border 2

10¼ yards binding length

8¼ yards lining/backing

* Always measure quilt top before cutting borders.
Borders are cut on the lengthwise grain.

12" ZIG THE ZAG BLOCK PATTERNS

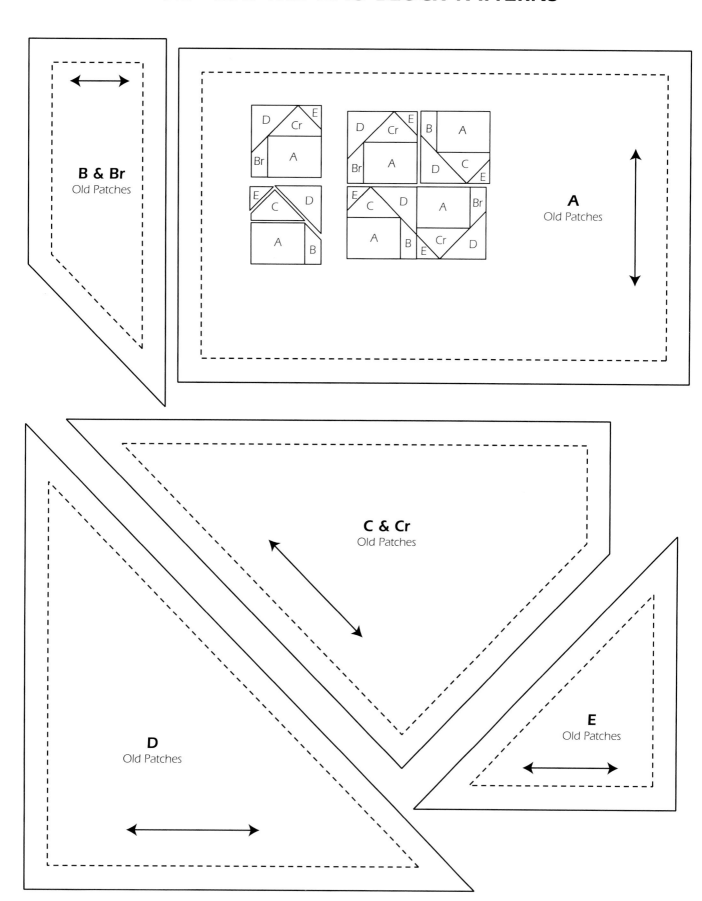

B & Br
Old Patches

A
Old Patches

C & Cr
Old Patches

D
Old Patches

E
Old Patches

CANDLES

Use 14" Zig the Zag block.
Patterns on pages 100–101

81" x 97" finished size
14" block
1¾" sashing
3" & 5" borders

New Classic Quilt Designs – Michal Mussell

CANDLES YARDAGES

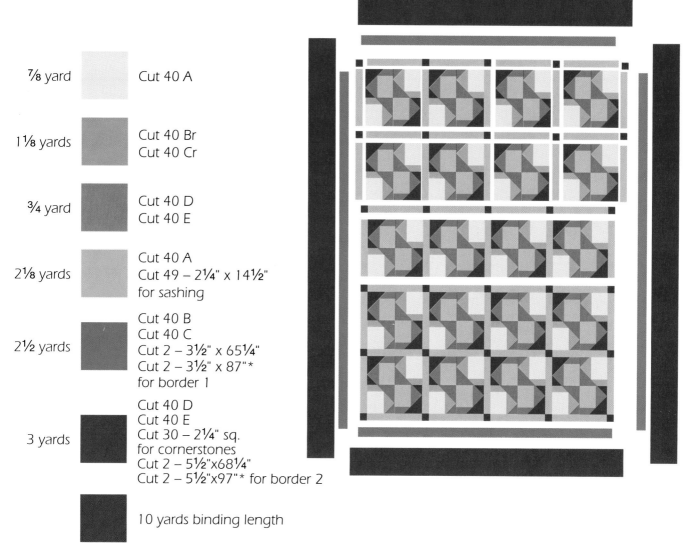

⅞ yard   Cut 40 A

1⅛ yards   Cut 40 Br
Cut 40 Cr

¾ yard   Cut 40 D
Cut 40 E

2⅛ yards   Cut 40 A
Cut 49 – 2¼" x 14½"
for sashing

2½ yards   Cut 40 B
Cut 40 C
Cut 2 – 3½" x 65¼"
Cut 2 – 3½" x 87"*
for border 1

3 yards   Cut 40 D
Cut 40 E
Cut 30 – 2¼" sq.
for cornerstones
Cut 2 – 5½"x68¼"
Cut 2 – 5½"x97"* for border 2

10 yards binding length

5½ yards for lining/backing

* Always measure quilt top before cutting borders.
Borders are cut on the lengthwise grain.

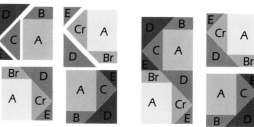

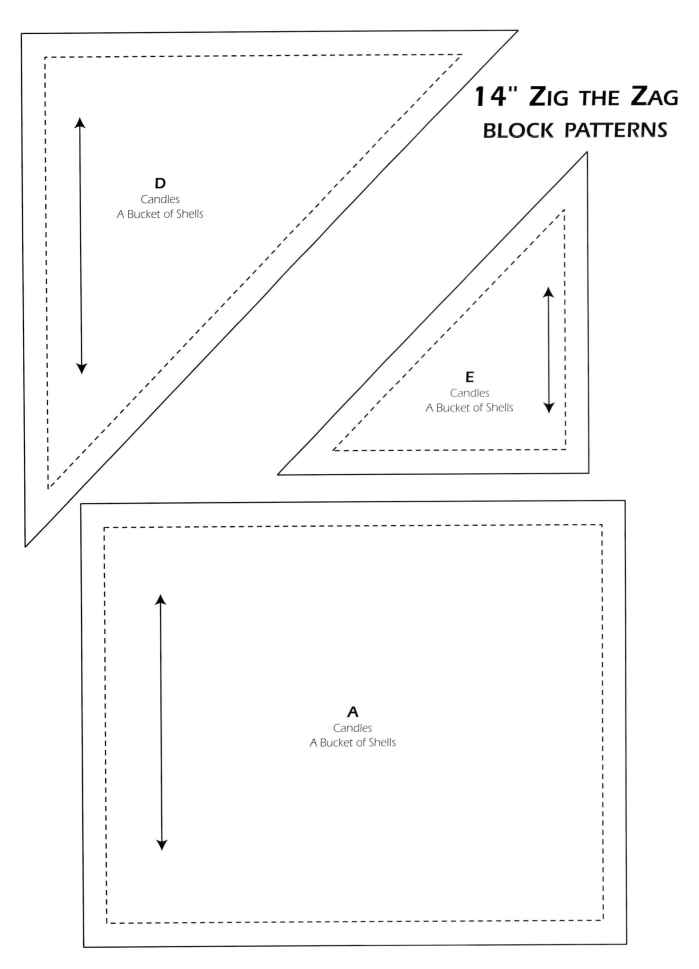

14" ZIG THE ZAG
BLOCK PATTERNS

D
Candles
A Bucket of Shells

E
Candles
A Bucket of Shells

A
Candles
A Bucket of Shells

14" ZIG THE ZAG BLOCK PATTERNS

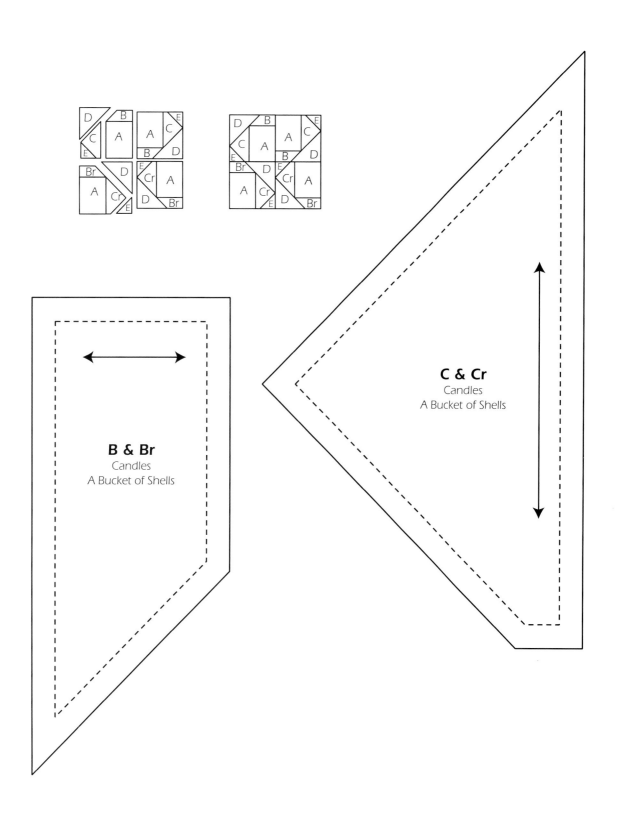

B & Br
Candles
A Bucket of Shells

C & Cr
Candles
A Bucket of Shells

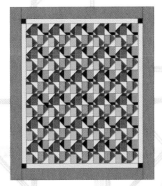

A BUCKET OF SHELLS

Use 14" Zig the Zag block.

Patterns on pages 100–101

90" x 104" finished size
14" blocks
3" & 7" borders

New Classic Quilt Designs – Michal Mussell

A Bucket of Shells Yardages

3½ yards — Cut 120 D
Cut 2 – 3½" x 70½"
Cut 2 – 3½" x 84½"*
for border 1

½ yard — Cut 120 E

¾ yard — Cut 30 B
Cut 30 C

¾ yard — Cut 30 Br
Cut 30 Cr

¾ yard — Cut 30 B
Cut 30 C

¾ yard — Cut 30 Br
Cut 30 Cr
Cut 4 – 3½" sq.
for cornerstones

¾ yard — Cut 30 A

¾ yard — Cut 30 A

¾ yard — Cut 30 A

¾ yard — Cut 30 A

3 yards
Cut length
of grain — Cut 2 – 7½" x 76½"
Cut 2 – 7½" x 104½"*
for border 2

11 yards binding length

9 yards lining/backing

* Always measure quilt top before cutting borders.
Borders are cut on the lengthwise grain.

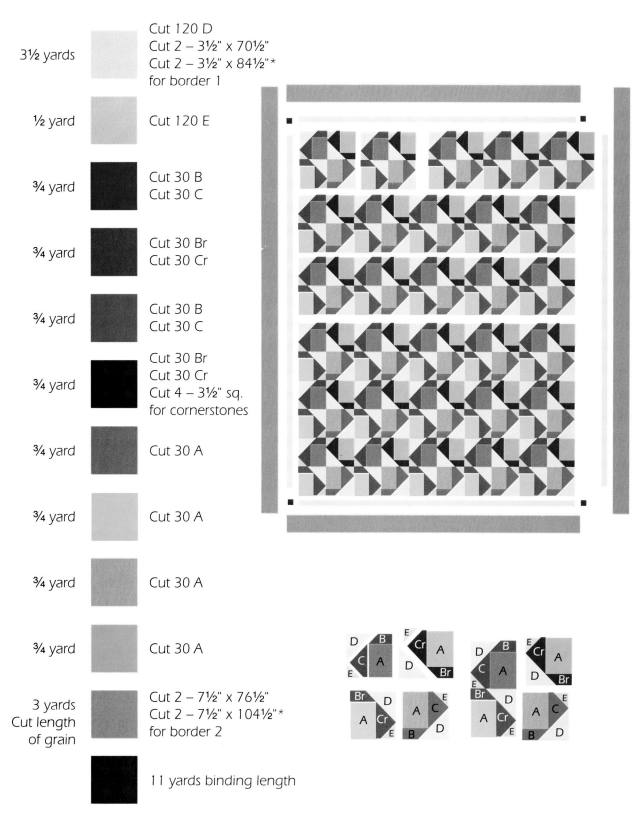

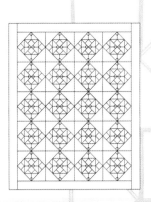

PRETTY IN PINK

Use To The Center block.

Patterns on page 107

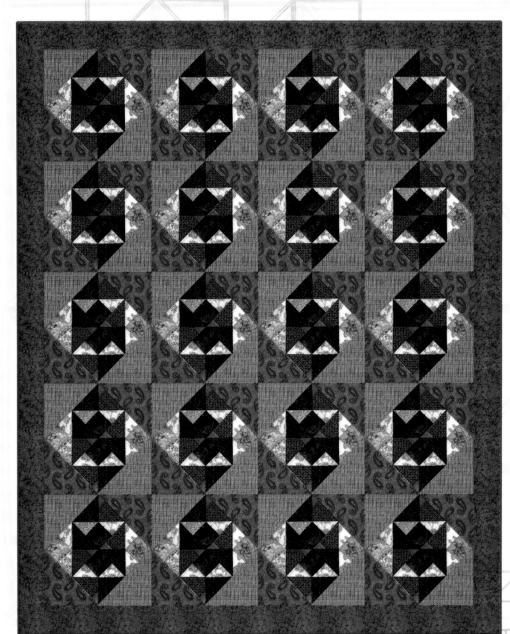

92" x 111" finished size
14" block
6" border

New Classic Quilt Designs – Michal Mussell

To The Center block

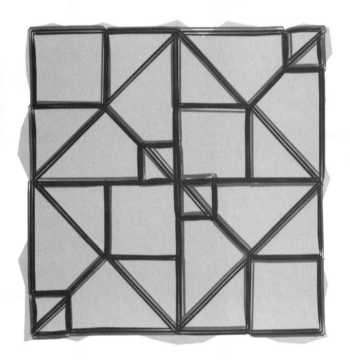

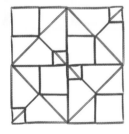 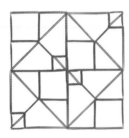 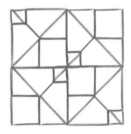

PRETTY IN PINK YARDAGES

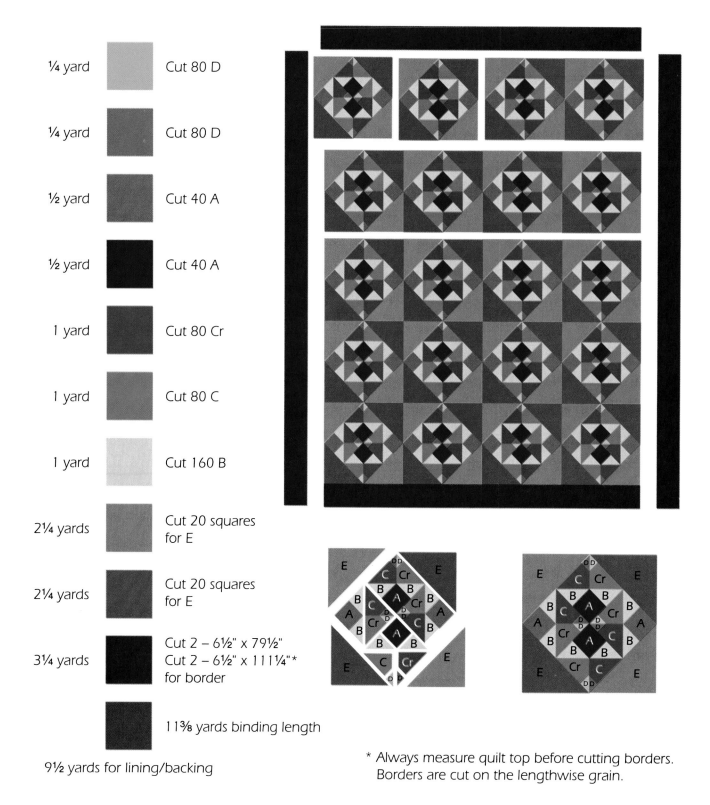

¼ yard — Cut 80 D

¼ yard — Cut 80 D

½ yard — Cut 40 A

½ yard — Cut 40 A

1 yard — Cut 80 Cr

1 yard — Cut 80 C

1 yard — Cut 160 B

2¼ yards — Cut 20 squares for E

2¼ yards — Cut 20 squares for E

3¼ yards — Cut 2 – 6½" x 79½"
Cut 2 – 6½" x 111¼"*
for border

11⅜ yards binding length

9½ yards for lining/backing

* Always measure quilt top before cutting borders.
Borders are cut on the lengthwise grain.

With the E triangle added, block measures 19¹³⁄₁₆".

TO THE CENTER BLOCK PATTERNS

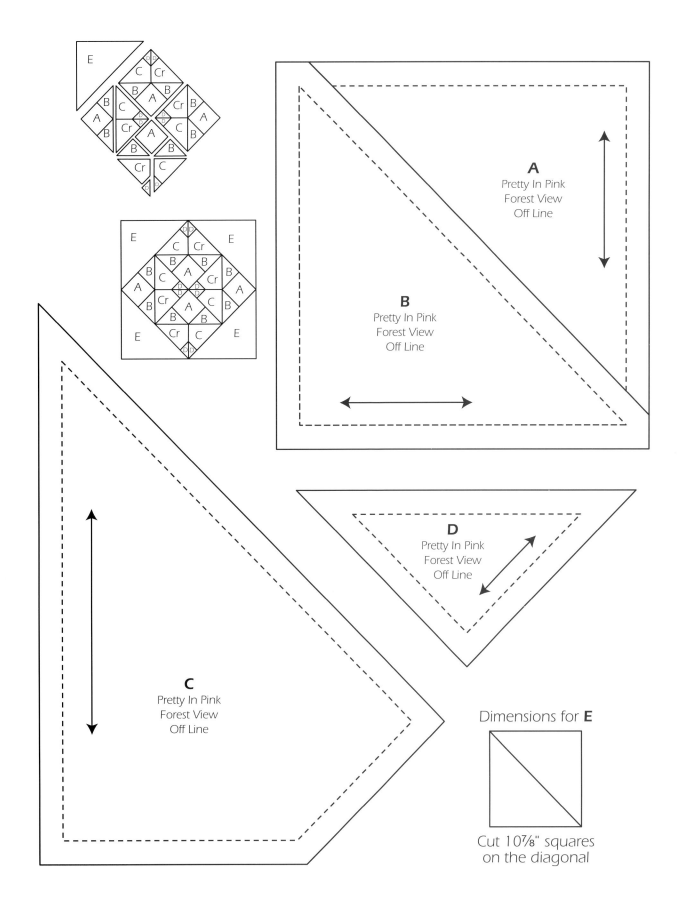

A
Pretty In Pink
Forest View
Off Line

B
Pretty In Pink
Forest View
Off Line

C
Pretty In Pink
Forest View
Off Line

D
Pretty In Pink
Forest View
Off Line

Dimensions for **E**

Cut 10⅞" squares
on the diagonal

FOREST VIEW

Use To The Center block.
Patterns on page 107

78" x 94" finished size
14" block
2" sashing
6" border

New Classic Quilt Designs – Michal Mussell

FOREST VIEW YARDAGES

¼ yard — Cut 80 D

¼ yard — Cut 80 D

1 yard — Cut 160 B

1¼ yards — Cut 80 C
Cut 30 – 2½" sq.
for cornerstones

1 yard — Cut 80 Cr

½ yard — Cut 40 A

2¾ yards — Cut 40 A
Cut 2 – 6½" x 66½"
Cut 2 – 6½" x 94½"*
for border

1¾ yards — Cut 49 – 2½" x 14½"
for sashing

9⅝ yards binding length

5¾ yards for lining/backing

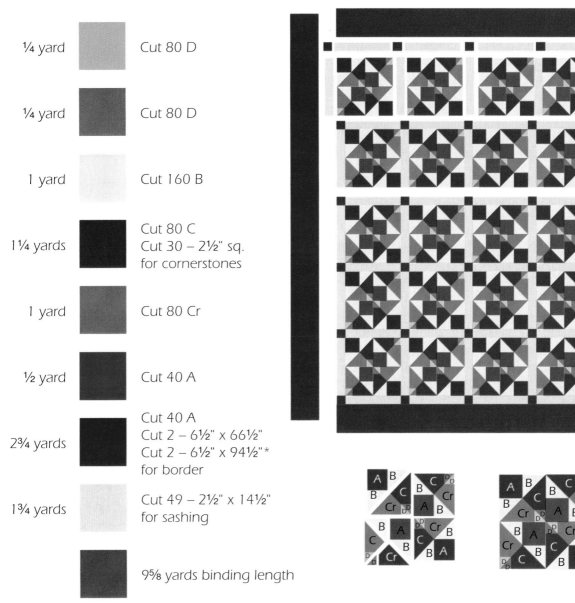

* Always measure quilt top before cutting borders.
Borders are cut on the lengthwise grain.

OFF LINE

Use To The Center block.

Patterns on page 107

74" x 88" finished size
14" block
3" & 6" borders

New Classic Quilt Designs – Michal Mussell

OFF LINE YARDAGES

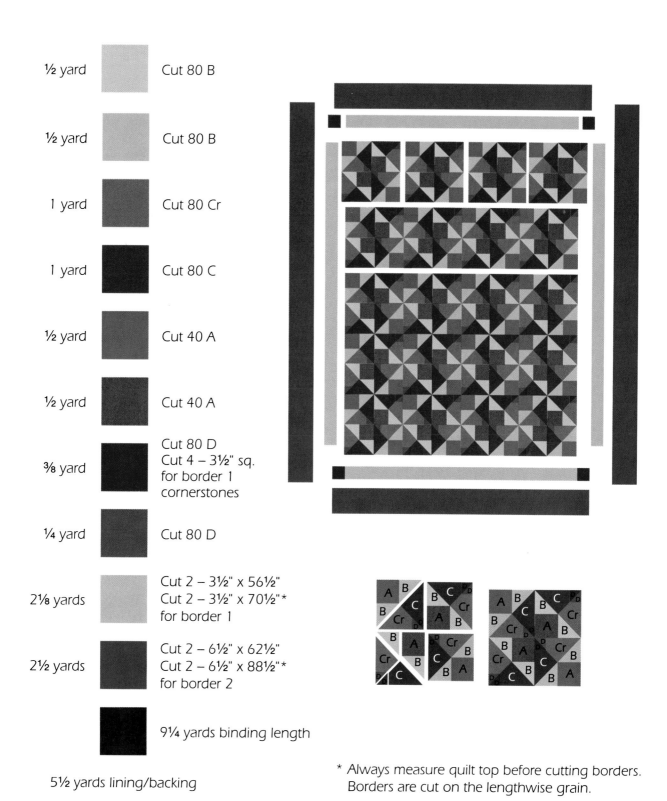

½ yard — Cut 80 B

½ yard — Cut 80 B

1 yard — Cut 80 Cr

1 yard — Cut 80 C

½ yard — Cut 40 A

½ yard — Cut 40 A

⅜ yard — Cut 80 D
Cut 4 – 3½" sq.
for border 1
cornerstones

¼ yard — Cut 80 D

2⅛ yards — Cut 2 – 3½" x 56½"
Cut 2 – 3½" x 70½"*
for border 1

2½ yards — Cut 2 – 6½" x 62½"
Cut 2 – 6½" x 88½"*
for border 2

9¼ yards binding length

5½ yards lining/backing

* Always measure quilt top before cutting borders.
Borders are cut on the lengthwise grain.

#4995 ▪ $19.95

This is only a small selection of the books available from the American Quilter's Society. AQS books are known worldwide for timely topics, clear writing, beautiful color photos, and accurate illustrations and patterns. The following books are available from your local bookseller, quilt shop, or public library.

#5176 ▪ $22.95

#4595 ▪ $18.95

#4545 ▪ $18.95

#4897 ▪ $19.95

#4889 ▪ $19.95

#3927 ▪ $12.95

#4627 ▪ $16.95

#4956 ▪ $19.95

Look for these books nationally or call 1-800-626-5420